Don't Do It
the Hard Way

2020 Edition

Your Uncle Ralph

Delvin R. Chatterson

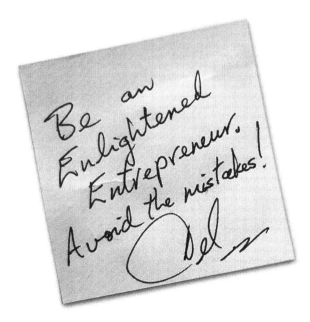

The Complete Do-It-Yourself Guide to Business Plans

4.5 Stars on Amazon

"Comprehensive and thorough, for a bullet proof business plan."

"Being a diehard Entrepreneur myself, I thought the books to be excellent reads and very informative and helpful for any aspiring Entrepreneur."

"Not boring like most other books of this type. For a solid business plan and many other good points to avoid basic mistakes when starting a business."

Don't Do It the Hard Way

5 Stars on Amazon

"Great book. Well written and an easy read. … a wealth of business experience distilled into easy to understand lessons. I liked his chapter on Managing in Difficult times - Stay focused, be relevant, look for opportunities in the crisis and leverage it to create urgency."

"I would strongly recommend reading this book, but most importantly learning from other's mistakes. A very good read and really great advice."

"What I like the most about both books is that we can immediately apply these ideas and keep on fixing what has to be fixed."

"Very complete and comprehensive, whether for the start-up entrepreneur, or small business people at any stage of their careers. I like the format - a great approach to get important lessons across - worthy of being reviewed regularly to assure that your ideas, strategies and tactics are being implemented.

Great information and the stories are a bonus. For someone like me that is going to start-up a business this book gives you the push you need. Stop shopping around and buy this book now.

For more advice on preparing a business plan to start, grow or exit your business:

The Complete Do-It-Yourself Guide to Business Plans
2020 Edition
Get the results you want

For more from Del Chatterson and your *Uncle Ralph* visit the websites or join the mailing lists at:

> LearningEntrepreneurship.com

> DelvinChatterson.com

Or follow on social media:

- Facebook: Author – Delvin Chatterson
- Instagram: Delvin R. Chatterson, Author
- LinkedIn: Del Chatterson
- Twitter: @ Del_UncleRalph

No Easy Money

You never win playing by the rules...

First in the series of Dale Hunter crime novels, No Easy Money is an explosive mix of crime, cash and computers in the 1980s. Dale Hunter is a young entrepreneur in the computer business under threats of violence from the Montreal Mafia. He wants to survive and not play by gangster rules, but it will require courage and creativity and the support of some new friends. Somebody is going to get killed.

Simply the Best

It may be simple, it's never easy

Dale Hunter is back in business, but so is Gino Boncanno. Hunter has already had to save himself from a murder attempt by the gangster, Boncanno. Now his new partner in Taiwan introduces him to the Triads and their smuggling schemes into the U.S. The danger escalates and Hunter still has to save himself and his family from the murderous plans of Boncanno. It may be simple, but it's never easy.

Merger Maniac

Some offers have to be refused

Third in the series, Merger Maniac is the story of how Dale Hunter is trying to thrive in the rapidly evolving computer business of the 1980s. He's looking for merger partners, but has to escape the aggressive and violent Montreal Mafia, who want him to join their money laundering schemes and are making very persuasive offers. Hunter has to walk a dangerous tightrope to avoid using their dirty money and getting dragged into more crime and corruption.

Don't Do It
the Hard Way

"A wise man learns from the mistakes of others.
Only a fool insists on making his own."

2020 EDITION

Your Uncle Ralph

Delvin R. Chatterson

Don't Do It the Hard Way
2020 Edition

ISBN softcover: 978-0-9879569-4-1
ISBN EPUB: 978-0-9879569-5-8
ISBN MOBI: 978-0-9879569-6-5

Advance release – March 2020
Final release – September 2020

Disclaimer: Throughout this book, the actual names and business details have been changed to protect the subjects of each story. Any apparent use of real names is purely coincidental.

For volume purchases or quantity discounts please contact the Author or Publisher directly.

Published by:
Uncle Ralph's Publishing Empire
www.LearningEntrepreneurship.com
(A division of 146152 Canada Inc.)
&
Canam Books/Rapido Press

*Dedicated to the principle that enlightened entrepreneurs
do better for themselves and their businesses
by also doing better for their families and employees,
their customers, suppliers and business partners,
their communities and the planet.*

Be better. Do better.

GUIDE TO THE CONTENTS

PART IV. Enlightened Entrepreneurship

PART V. Random Ramblings from your Uncle Ralph

PART VI. References & Checklists

Can Uncle Ralph help you do better?

As a cautious and skeptical entrepreneur, and before you spend your valuable time and money on this 2020 edition of DON'T DO IT THE HARD WAY, you should be asking whether it is going to help you avoid making mistakes in your business.

How can Del Chatterson, your Uncle Ralph, help? What does he know about avoiding the mistakes? Does he really have important and valuable ideas, information and inspiration for entrepreneurs?

I think so, but you'll have to decide for yourself. Then after you've looked at these stories entrepreneur-to-entrepreneur, please let me know what you think and whether you have any questions for me.

My intent, as your Uncle Ralph, is to share my knowledge and experience in entrepreneurship. We all learn from our mistakes, but it's also important to learn from the mistakes of others. We don't have to make them all ourselves – life is too short!

This book is based on the principle that entrepreneurs learn best by sharing stories with other entrepreneurs. In it I share my own stories, including the mistakes I've made, and the stories of other entrepreneurs who have also learned from their mistakes. Of course, occasionally we get it right and I'll share what we've learned from those experiences too.

Some of the most important lessons in DON'T DO IT THE HARD WAY will help you with these challenges:

- *Getting Started*
  When and how? Can you succeed as an entrepreneur?

- *Strategic Leadership plus Management Effectiveness*
  The biggest challenge for every entrepreneur is to provide strategic leadership while managing effectively.

- *Managing Relationships*
  Building and maintaining strong and effective relationships with employees, customers, suppliers, business partners and the bank.

- *Managing the Numbers*
  Understanding the basic principles of finance and achieving sustainable profitable growth.

- *Marketing, Sales and Customer Service*
  Three essential elements that must be done well to build loyal, long-term, profitable customer relationships.

- *Building Business Value*
  Achieving more than simple profitability, but long term business value from the start-up to your exit.

If I can inspire and inform you on these issues, I will have succeeded in helping you to learn from the mistakes of others and avoid making too many of your own.

Avoid the mistakes
Don't Do It the Hard Way

Introduction to your Uncle Ralph

DEL CHATTERSON IS YOUR UNCLE RALPH

As you have invested your time and money in this book you have a right to know, "Who is Uncle Ralph and how can he help me and my business?"

So here is my story.

I am your "Uncle Ralph". You can call me Del.

I am an entrepreneur and business consultant, writer, golfer, photographer, happy husband, proud father and grandfather. Originally a small town boy from the Rocky Mountains of Western Canada, I have lived, worked or visited every province and territory in Canada, all fifty states of the U.S., most of Western Europe, parts of Asia and Central America. My home for most of the past forty-plus years has been the fascinating, multicultural, bilingual, French-Canadian city of Montreal. I did my MBA at McGill in Montreal a few years after graduating as an Engineer from UBC in Vancouver.

I have extensive experience in the corporate world, in management consulting and as an entrepreneur in my own businesses. My early corporate experience included financial analysis and systems integration projects, purchasing and materials management with Alcan Aluminum and AES Data. I spent six years with Coopers and Lybrand in management consulting, working with businesses mostly in Canada, but also in Europe and Central America. As an independent business consultant, I have worked with many entrepreneurs and business owners, often clients of the Business Development Bank of Canada (BDC).

In recent years, I have gained more international business exposure as a Volunteer Advisor with CESO (Canadian Executive Services Overseas), an agency providing aid to developing economies in Africa, Asia and South America and to Aboriginal communities in Canada. It has been enlightening to share my business ideas and solutions with entrepreneurs in these exceptionally challenging environments of widespread poverty, untrained workers and limited infrastructure. It has provided a very striking affirmation of the extremely favourable economic and political environments in North America where most of us work.

My most significant experience as an entrepreneur and business owner was with TTX Computer Products, an import and distribution business in Montreal. It was about two years after my last corporate job imploded and I had decided to avoid letting that ever happen again. I wanted to manage my own career plan and started looking for opportunities to start a business while working as an independent consultant. A project in Toronto developing a specialized educational computer led me to an introduction to TTX computer monitors and the opening of my own distribution business in Montreal. I was able to grow it from zero in 1986 to a $20 million-a-year business with distribution centres in Montreal and Boston within eight years. And I learned a lot about entrepreneurship.

I then took the business into and out of a corporate merger for some more difficult lessons in entrepreneurship.

My next start-up adventure was with a technology partner in an early e-commerce business called nxtNet Inc. We got off to a good start, but when the dot-com bubble burst, we wrapped it up like so many other technology businesses and came up with a new plan. The learning experience continued.

Over the past twenty years I have also continued to manage my consulting business, DirectTech Solutions, working with entrepreneurs to help them respond to their business challenges and realize their opportunities.

I have assisted entrepreneurs and owner-managed businesses in a wide variety of industries at different stages of their business life cycle. The challenges ranged from start-up and growth plans, to improving strategic direction and financial performance, to marketing and sales management, cash flow and organisation issues through to planning their exit strategies.

I have also given courses, lectures and workshops in Entrepreneurship, Finance and Business Planning at both Concordia and McGill universities in Montreal and in other businesses and organizations internationally.

Your Uncle Ralph comes from all of that experience. He is also influenced by my father's good advice and example and by everything I have learned from the many good, bad and indifferent, managers that I have worked with over the years. Not entirely coincidentally, Ralph is my secret middle name and was my father's first name. Uncle Ralph is definitely much wiser than I am and has experienced more than I could possibly have lived through myself. He is my alter ego when writing for entrepreneurs.

Uncle Ralph's interest is to share his ideas, experience and advice with other entrepreneurs to help improve their businesses and their lives. Of course, I will continue to learn in the process too.

All this knowledge and experience has been incorporated into the writing of this book. My intent is to help entrepreneurs everywhere to learn more and to do better; better for themselves, their families, employees, customers and suppliers; their communities and the planet.

Please enjoy reading the book and sharing the ideas with other entrepreneurs.

Be better. Do better.

Your Uncle Ralph

Del Chatterson

March 2020

Introduction to Learning Entrepreneurship

Entrepreneurs learn to be better and do better in the same way that other people do – they learn from examples and they listen to their peers.

Learning from textbooks can provide an initial understanding of the fundamentals of business and management, but grinding through textbooks is very unappealing to the action-oriented, over-worked and often document-challenged entrepreneur.

We can also learn and be inspired by others – the celebrity entrepreneurs like Steve Jobs, Richard Branson, Mark Zuckerberg, or whoever your star entrepreneur may be. But the lessons learned may not be relevant and their experiences just do not fit the circumstances of most entrepreneurs – those of us who are not yet billionaires and have no corporate jet to visit operations around the world. Maybe it's useful to visualize those success stories as your long-term objective, but don't get stuck in the daydream.

Let's start with the lessons that are most applicable to your current challenges and opportunities – lessons learned by small business owners like you.

In my experience, entrepreneurs get their most valuable input from exchanges with other entrepreneurs. It may be over coffee or lunch, in business meetings, industry associations, networking events and conferences, or peer advisory groups like the **e2eForum** that I describe in this book.

The e2eForum is based on my personal experience with two very successful peer advisory groups that I initiated.

The first was the Professional Services Network (PSN), a group of about twelve professional advisors and consultants, including an accountant, lawyer and banker – business owners and independent professionals who offered services not products, to businesses not consumers. We had a lot in common and helped each other in many ways – sharing tips and tools, market feedback, strategies and tactics on management, marketing and financing. We occasionally brought in guest speakers to add to the exchange and often worked together on joint projects or promotion of our services. The regular meetings allowed us to extend our networks, knowledge and experience with a group of trusted and competent peers in a confidential, non-competitive environment.

The second initiative was a Strategic Roundtable for entrepreneurs. The approach was to invite a group of current clients to share their stories, current challenges, good and bad experiences and lessons learned. They were all business owners from very different businesses and were surprised to discover how many issues they had in common; in sales management, bank relations, business development or exit strategies. There were no direct competitors, customers or suppliers in the group so all the participants were comfortable discussing their failures and concerns, as well as their achievements.

Some participants were more open than others and some talked too much. But it was an eye-opening experience for everyone; providing new ideas and generating new confidence in their ability to find solutions. My objective here is to accomplish the same for you.

Please join me, your Uncle Ralph, in the exchange of ideas, information and inspiration with other entrepreneurs in the e2eForum. After reading these stories, you might want to find an e2eForum near you or start one yourself. You will find more information on how to organize an e2eForum in **Part VI – References and Checklists**.

To learn more about entrepreneurship and how to be successful with your business you may also find it useful to visit my website: **LearningEntrepreneurship.com**

PART I
Sharing Stories
Entrepreneur to Entrepreneur

1 **Meet the Members of our e2eForum**

The **e2eForum** is a group of entrepreneurs sharing ideas, information and inspiration. They meet regularly for breakfast and discuss the issues in each of their businesses – how to avoid the mistakes, how to be better and do better.

In the following chapters you will meet these members of the e2e-Forum:

Larry – a young computer engineer leaving his day job soon to work on a mobile app for monitoring health and fitness.

Vivian – a veterinarian and pet store owner, trying to grow from her single retail location into a national franchised business.

Brian – an entrepreneur and the owner of a business providing Web development and e-commerce services.

Stan – the second generation owner of a small contracting business that installs and maintains heating and ventilation equipment.

Dave – an engineer, MBA and former corporate executive, now running an importing and distribution business for high performance bicycles.

Paul – age 57, an experienced entrepreneur running a machine shop and thinking about his exit strategy.

… plus occasional guests and me, your **Uncle Ralph**.

Welcome to our Meeting

WHY ARE YOU HERE?

"Why do you want to be an entrepreneur in the first place?"

Paul, the most experienced entrepreneur in the group, was asking the question of Larry, the young start-up entrepreneur, because he was getting tired of listening to Larry's continual complaints. Nothing was going as planned. He was having no fun and still not making any money.

And it was a good question. Most of us ask it of ourselves occasionally and we all have different answers. Why does anyone want to be an entrepreneur?

Larry had probably asked himself the question recently too, but now we were all wondering the same thing.

"If it's going so badly in your new business, why would you ever quit your day job? Maybe it's time to give it up and just work harder on your corporate career."

"Hell no," said Larry. "My own business may not always be fun or profitable, but it will always be better than that."

We all agreed.

"Right," said Stan, "I may be a lousy manager, but I'm still the best boss I ever had. And it sure beats working for somebody else."

Vivian added, "And it's so satisfying to make your own decisions, then live with the results, good or bad."

"OK, so let's talk about how we got started in business and why," I said.

"It will help Larry's thinking and give us all a good reminder of why we're entrepreneurs in the first place. A good way to start the day – unless we decide someone made a mistake and shouldn't ever be an entrepreneur at all!"

So we adjusted the day's agenda based on the discussion already started. (Not the first time we'd done that.)

WELCOME TO THE E2EFORUM

We're a group of entrepreneurs that meet regularly – every third Thursday of the month over breakfast from 7:30AM to 9:00AM, to miss rush-hour traffic but before missing any of the work day.

I had started this group about six months ago with **Paul**, the owner of a machine shop who had done well for over twenty years and was now thinking of his retirement. We both valued the opportunity to share ideas and experiences with other entrepreneurs, especially in a quiet, confidential environment without any conflicting or competing interests. I had the experience of organizing similar peer advisory groups in the past.

In a few weeks, we had added other members and now there were seven of us, including me and Paul. We all come from different businesses and are at different stages in the business life cycle. You will get to know us all better in the next few meetings.

The newest entrepreneur is **Larry**, a young computer engineer planning to leave his day job soon to launch a mobile app for monitoring personal health and fitness. He has developed an initial version and is test marketing it with free downloads. He's still drafting his business plan, while starting to develop connections with potential strategic partners and sources of financing. He's at the very early-stage of starting his own business.

Vivian is a veterinarian and pet store owner. She has run her own pet store and clinic for about six years and is very dedicated to healthy, personalized pet care. She is now trying to develop and expand her single suburban location into a franchised business model and expand it across the country.

Brian is also a young entrepreneur, but has been running a Web development and e-commerce business since leaving university four years ago. He had discovered his aptitude for computer science in high school when he started designing his own computer games. But he also impresses us with his ability to manage the complexities of the technology and the demands of operating his business while still maintaining a strategic focus on his long-term plan to stay ahead of the competition.

Stan is the second generation owner of a small contracting business specializing in commercial heating and ventilation equipment. His father started the business as an independent contractor installing heating and air conditioning equipment in residential construction projects and eventually grew his business to twelve employees working on more advanced industrial projects. Stan started working with his father after high school and acquired all the necessary technical training and certifications, but he struggles with management of the business after his father passed away two years ago and he had to take over as the owner-manager.

Dave is a forty-something engineer, MBA and former corporate executive, now running an importing and distribution business for high performance bicycles. He made the leap when his career plan needed a jolt and his employer offered only more of the same. He was introduced by a fellow cyclist to a new high performance bicycle brand from Italy that was looking for distribution in North America. The opportunity fit with Dave's management experience and it got him excited enough to put in a big chunk of his own money and sign personal guarantees for a bank line of credit to get started. Now in his third year, he's facing challenges to manage both the supply from the bicycle manufacturer and the financing from the bank to keep up with his rapid sales growth.

The entire group was in attendance this morning and had now agreed on the following revised agenda.

Start-up questions
- **When to leap?**
- **What do you need before you start?**
- **Who will succeed and who will not?**
- **Why and why not?**

All very philosophical questions, but necessary to think about – before, during and after any entrepreneurial adventure.

Larry started with the first question, "So how did you get started as an entrepreneur, Uncle Ralph?"

"Well," I replied, "I often say that starting your own business is a lot like sky-diving – it seems like an exciting idea, but you're not likely to do it until you're pushed out the door.

"In my case, I had literally been pushed out the door of a technology company, called AES Data, which was winding down when my number came up. Not a surprise, since I had spent the previous nine months closing facilities and letting people go, but it was a painful experience nonetheless. I quickly had two other corporate job offers from Nortel and Rolls Royce in Montreal, both with similar job descriptions and compensation packages to what I had at AES, but I decided it was time to take care of my own career plan and not let someone else decide whether I had a job and what I was doing next.

"Besides, with an MBA and lots of experience, I was ready to prove that I was at least as good a manager and businessman as the people I had been working for. So I went back to consulting on my own and started to explore opportunities to start in business for myself.

"That's when I met the owners of TTX, a brand of computer monitors, who were looking for a distributor in Eastern Canada. That appealed to me because it matched my interests in technology and I had good credentials in managing the distribution side of a business. So I quit consulting, put in some cash and agreed to start with no salary as we opened a joint venture distribution business in Montreal. It was a great experience from the first day."

As I looked around the table, I realized that we had all arrived at entrepreneurship from different backgrounds and got started at different times in our lives, but we were all attracted for the same reasons.

The attractions that we usually agreed on were these:

- Unlimited opportunity to go where you want whenever you want
- Freedom and independence to do things your way
- Continuous challenge and variety of experience
- Responsibility for all facets of the business
- Control over both your career and your choices of work/life balance.

However, being an entrepreneur quickly leads you to recognize the less attractive elements of that career choice too:

- There are still limits to what you can do or can control
- Many more people are now dependent on you for their own success
- The business requires skills and knowledge that you probably do not have
- Your work does not get left at the office
- You now have more at risk and less financial security.

Other entrepreneurs have made some memorable observations that highlight the contradictions:

"I used to work for someone I called the boss. Now I work for thirty people who call me boss."

"I wanted to be my own boss. But now I have many bosses – my customers, my employees, my suppliers, the bank, the landlord, the government and the city! It's hard to satisfy them all."

"It's still better than working for somebody else."

"I'm the best boss I ever had!"

Which can you say about yourself and your business?

CAN YOU SUCCEED AS AN ENTREPRENEUR?

Although you may still be attracted to entrepreneurship, will you succeed? What does it take to be a successful entrepreneur?

It was Vivian who asked the next question, "Is there really an *entrepreneurial type*? What are the personal characteristics, attitudes and abilities that are essential to success? You've worked with a lot of entrepreneurs, Uncle Ralph, surely you've learned to recognize who will succeed and who will not."

"Sorry, but it's never that obvious to me or anybody else that I know of. Unfortunately, there is no easy stereotype that applies."

I added, "And if we define success as running a business with continuing growth and profitability, then we also have to admit that success is not always entirely due to the owner-manager.

"I would argue that although *failure is always the fault of bad management; success is not always the result of good management*. Success also requires good luck and good market conditions.

"Even with good management your business may fail. Not a pleasant prospect, but an important truth. We'll talk about it another day, but my theory is that it's more important to avoid catastrophic failure than it is to chase big success stories. Manage for the small victories that will eventually add up to a big success story. We'll discuss it further when I present *The Seven Biggest Mistakes that Entrepreneurs Make* and how they can be avoided.

"However, back to Vivian's question, there are some common characteristics of successful entrepreneurs that you can check off for yourself.

Here is my short checklist of the ***Characteristics of a Successful Entrepreneur***:

- ❏ Energetic, competitive
- ❏ Independent, confident, determined
- ❏ Action-oriented, decisive
- ❏ Passionate, persuasive.

"If you don't have them all yourself, then you better include a partner in your plans."

DON'T QUIT YOUR DAY JOB YET

Then I continued, "Before you leap into the unknowns of entrepreneurship, you need to go through another checklist, starting with your *Basic Defensive Interval*."

This time Larry spoke up, "Now I'm getting worried, I haven't got a checklist and I've never even heard of the Basic Defensive Interval."

"Not to worry," I said. "I had to have it explained to me too, the first time I was asked about it. It simply means: *How long can you last without income?*

"If you quit your day job today, but you still need $3000 a month to live on and you only have $15,000 in the bank, then your Basic Defensive Interval is five months. After that, if your new business cannot afford to pay you at least $3000 a month, then you better have a new day job!

"OK," said Larry, "so if I need six months to get my business up to speed and I need $5000 a month to live on, then I have to have at least $30,000 in the bank before I quit my day job?"

"Right, but you also have to have enough additional financing beyond the $30,000 required for your living expenses to invest in the start-up of your business."

"Got it. If I need another $50,000 for operating costs, sales and marketing expenses, before we generate sufficient revenue in the business to cover them, then I'll need a cash reserve of $80,000 before launching. That makes it clearer what I need to arrange for financing."

"You definitely need to know the financing required before you start, but there is a longer checklist."

I went to the flipchart and wrote:

The Before You Start Checklist

- ❑ Skills, knowledge, experience, and contacts relevant to your business plan.
- ❑ Expectations and preferences for the entrepreneurial lifestyle – work routine and environment, prestige and compensation, work/life balance.
- ❑ Personal strengths and weaknesses that will help, not hurt, the business.
- ❑ A healthy foundation – family, physical and financial. Solid not shaky.

❑ Strategic resources in place – partners, suppliers, facilities, key customers and employees.

❑ Financing required for start-up – covering your Basic Defensive Interval and the first few months of negative cash flow.

"If you can't put a checkmark with confidence in every box, then you better try harder – recognize the deficiencies and fill in the gaps. Maybe you require more time to develop your skills and get more relevant experience or to beef up your foundation and resources before launching."

"Ouch," said Stan. "Now I know why it's been so hard taking over from my father. I just wasn't ready. I'm still missing check marks on a lot of those points."

Others were nodding and taking notes. It was time to wind up this e2eForum meeting. I asked if everyone was satisfied that we had adequately covered the key discussion points on choosing entrepreneurship and getting ready to start a new business.

"I think we're good," said Vivian. "I've got to get to work and review that last checklist. There are some important elements missing for me too. I'll get started now on making the adjustments.

"See you soon everybody. Have a good day!"

Starting-Up is Hard to Do

INITIAL DECISIONS DEFINE THE DIRECTION

We were gathered again for our Thursday morning e2eForum meeting and everyone was getting settled.

As usual, Larry was carefully maneuvering his over-laden breakfast plate to the table with a coffee in one hand, the plate and utensils in the other and a notebook clamped under his arm. A single guy, it was apparently his best breakfast of the week and he was making the most of it. The others were usually more discrete with a small healthy plate of food and a large cup of coffee.

Brian was the chairperson today and he was writing on the flipchart:

Start-up Decisions
- **Strategic Positioning**
- **Strategic Partnerships**
- **Business model choices**
- **Document requirements**

He sat at the head of the table, giving me a wink to confirm that he was using the list I had suggested.

"Last meeting we all found it useful to think back to when we were getting started in business," he said. "So I thought we should continue on that theme and discuss some of the other decisions that need to be made at the start-up stage."

Dave interjected, "Maybe we'll discover again that we've missed a few steps. Still, it's never too late to get them right."

"Absolutely," I said, "and even if you did make good decisions when you started, your environment will have changed since then and you may need to make new decisions now. At least once a year get out the *road map* that got you started, assuming you have one, called a *Business Plan*. Check whether you still have the same destination and that you're still happy with the route you chose, the bus you built and the passengers you're traveling with."

"OK," said Larry between mouthfuls, "the rest of you are far enough along to look back and do that review, but I'm just getting started. What are the first decisions to make?"

Since he was at a very early stage, I gave him the same suggestion I give to new entrepreneurs in my Business Planning class.

"Start by coming up with a name and a marketing slogan. That will help you define how you want to be seen by your customers when they compare you to all the competing alternatives they have.

"Defining yourself relative to the market is called **Strategic Positioning** and it's a very important early decision. Do you want to be seen as the IBM of your industry – competent professionals, or more like Disney – friendly and fun to do business with? Will your corporate image be that of prestige and performance like a sporty Porsche or of rugged utility like a hefty pick-up truck? Those decisions are an early requirement right after you've defined the business opportunity and chosen your business model – decisions on your strategic positioning and how you wish to be perceived by customers.

"But remember, your choice of strategic positioning will only be realized if it is communicated and demonstrated *consistently*. It should influence *everything* in your business – from office décor and business cards to your website design, sales rep's dress code and their automobile choices, customer service policies, product pricing and packaging. It's the starting point in defining your corporate culture."

Paul was the first to respond, "I have to admit that we arrived at our positioning and corporate culture by default, not by specific decisions. My history in machine shops gave me the experience and confidence to trust my instincts. I just did what seemed right to me whenever I had to make a decision. And now it's too late to change the stripes on this old tiger."

"Not an unusual approach, Paul," I replied. "Most entrepreneurs go by instinct and personal preference on these questions of strategy and corporate image. Consequently, the corporate personality is often very much a reflection of the owner's personality. Which is fine; if it's appropriate to the business and attractive to its prospective customers. If not, then the corporate image can probably still be presented favourably enough to attract business. Where it's more likely to be a big problem is when the owner's personal management style is applied throughout the business and causes the resulting corporate culture to negatively affect the attraction and management of both employees and customers."

There were some quiet nods around the table as they thought of their own familiar examples and my mind wandered back to my own worst experience.

CHOOSE YOUR PARTNERS WELL

After eight successful years of rapid growth and good profitability in computer products distribution, I had decided to expand and grow to the next level by entering into a merger with a new business partner. *What a disaster that turned out to be.*

Strategically, it made great sense – complementary product lines, expansion into more territories, a more balanced portfolio of customers and suppliers and great synergies in sales, marketing and administration.

But what I saw from the outside was not the same personality that was hidden inside my new partner's business. From the outside, it appeared to be a successful distribution business with high-value specialty products and good quality customers. I had known the owner for many years and we had done business together in the past. He was charming, knowledgeable and appeared to be managing his business well. But, as I often said afterwards, it was like thinking you know someone at the office, then discovering when you visit him at home that he kicks the dog and yells at his kids.

After the merger, I was exposed to his completely dysfunctional management style. Abusive, selfish, and paranoid; his employees feared him, never gave him any bad news and imitated his aggressive style among themselves. It was surprising that they had survived at all and it soon ended badly for the merger. A true personality conflict – both for the two companies and the two owners. Let's just say, 'We no longer do lunch.'

"Which leads us to the next important point," I said, coming out of my mental detour, "choosing good strategic partners."

"But I'm never going to have a partner," said Stan, "One thing my father insisted on – you can rely on your family, but never bring in a partner."

"But you already have **strategic partners**," I said, "Your key managers and your banker, your biggest customer and the major suppliers that you depend upon. You need to make good choices on them all. I didn't always and most of us have suffered the consequences of choosing some bad partners. So in spite of what your father said, let's talk about business partners that might be more valuable to your business than the available family members. Maybe even more trustworthy."

"Oh boy, have I got some stories for you," added Paul. "A brother-in-law and a nephew I wish I'd never met. We don't have time this morning for me to tell you the whole story about how my wife insisted they could help my business; then they almost put me out of business. Believe me, they're not allowed anywhere close to my shop anymore."

"No family in your exit strategy?" asked Dave.

"Only if I can adopt a bright, capable entrepreneur like you or Vivian," replied Paul. "Too bad you're both already occupied."

There were a few other mumbles around the table as conversations continued about bad experiences with family members getting involved in the business.

"Dealing with family members, though, is a good place to start setting the ground rules for everyone directly involved in your business," I suggested.

"*It's essential for every business to clearly define the roles and expectations of owners, and family members if there are any in the business, as **managers**, separately from their rights and obligations as **shareholders**.* Don't even start the business without signed shareholder agreements and key employee job descriptions and employment contracts.

"In the area of legal agreements and financial structure, you should seek professional advice from lawyers and accountants before making the classic entrepreneur's mistake of neglecting the necessary paperwork. Small omissions in these technicalities can get very expensive when the unexpected actually happens. It would be inappropriate for me to give you advice in those areas, but I do have a checklist you can use to cover the essentials."

"Oh good," said Larry as he pulled his notebook out from under his empty plate, "another checklist."

I smiled at him and flipped over the discussion page for today to start a new sheet, with the heading, *The Start-up Documents Checklist*, commenting on each point as I wrote:

1. **Business Plan.**
   "Often neglected, always necessary. And I wrote the book, as you know. For anyone who needs a copy of my *Do-It-Yourself Guide to Business Plans*, I always have one in my briefcase. I won't do the whole speech today, but you absolutely need to have a documented business plan for start-up, to manage the business successfully and to prepare for exit." (*Actually, that is pretty much the whole speech.*)

2. **Shareholder agreement.**
   "Include all the standard terms, but ensure you understand the buy/sell provisions, especially the 'shotgun' clause. You want to have a prior arrangement for any partner to buy in, buy more or sell out."

3. **Life insurance on each other.**
   "You don't want to suddenly have a dead partner and then find yourself working with an incompetent or unhelpful husband or wife as your new partner. Life insurance allows you to buy out your deceased partner's interest and avoid that unhappy arrangement."

4. **Incorporation.**
   "There are other business structures, such as a sole proprietorship or a partnership, but I always recommend incorporation to prove that you're serious about your business and have provided a structure to build on. Especially if you plan for your business to achieve more than give you a temporary, part-time job. Incorporate, so you can look like a world class multi-national before you become one."

5. **Business licenses and regulatory approvals.**
   "You'll be surprised how many regulations there are, whatever business you're in. And ignorance is no defense when the auditors and inspectors arrive. Do your homework and pay the fees; it's always cheaper than paying the penalties later."

6. **Information systems.**
   "Start by making good choices on your information systems. The essentials are an accounting, invoicing and management information system; office productivity tools for preparing documents, quotes and proposals; and a contact database or customer relationship management software for business development and customer service. These can amount to large initial investments on start-up, but if you decide to avoid them and start small, be sure that there is an upgrade path to support your growth to a world class business. You don't intend to stay small do you, Larry?" He had no comment, just a smug smile.

7. **Leases and contracts for facilities and services.**
   "Here you can make your own list depending on what you need for your particular business."

"OK," I concluded, "those are the essential documents for start-up. Now did everybody here do them all before they launched and announced to the world that they were in business?"

"Off course not," said Paul, as he looked around the table. "We all started knocking on doors before we had incorporated, written a business plan or had a first contract. Learn by doing, right Dave? Vivian?"

Even Brian was nodding sheepishly, as if it was an admission he was not as organized and cautious an entrepreneur as we all thought.

"That's my experience too," I admitted. "It usually takes a year into the business before you complete the checklist. But I'm sticking to the list as a minimum requirement for good management of your business."

Stan was starting to pack up for the office and left us with his action item for the day. "We've been in business for twenty-seven years and we've never completed the *Start-up Document Checklist*. It's on my To-Do List now!"

"Me too," said Paul. "Maybe a little late, but it will still help me put together everything I need before I launch my exit plan."

"The document list is good," said Brian, "but I'm more concerned about reviewing our strategic positioning. We have some notable inconsistencies in presenting our corporate image between the 'geeky technology experts' and the 'friendly helpful customer service reps,' so I'm going to look at our marketing campaigns and website to make it clearer that we are both competent and user friendly."

Stan added, "I also made some notes about our current strategic partners and we need to do some re-alignment there too."

"Sounds good," I said, "Lots to work on before the next meeting. See you then."

PART II
Avoid the Mistakes

Too Entrepreneurial?

IT'S NOT A GOOD THING

Brian was still chairing at the next meeting, but he had a look of concern; unusual for him, as he was normally upbeat and confident.

Gesturing to the flipchart, he said, "These are the issues that I'm worrying about and they're starting to wear me down. Mostly because my two senior managers are starting to tell me I'm not entrepreneurial enough."

We looked at his list.

Too Entrepreneurial?

- Opportunistic
- Optimistic
- Impatient
- Confident
- Decisive
- Creative

He added, "Uncle Ralph, when we were working together on my original business plan, you warned me about the risks of being too entrepreneurial. These are the points I remember and I thought we could discuss them today in the e2eForum."

"But those points all look good to me," said Stan. "My father was always pushing me to be more like that."

"It all comes down to balance," I said. "Balancing the entrepreneurial instincts and drive with the well thought-out strategic planning and analysis that will help you make good decisions."

"Let's go through the list," said Vivian, keeping us on the agenda.

I opened by explaining my perception that although certain characteristics of entrepreneurs are necessary for them to be successful. Too entrepreneurial can be a problem for the business.

I went over the points that I had previously discussed with Brian, while we worked on his business plan and he was bubbling with entrepreneurial enthusiasm. My intent was not to dampen his energy and enthusiasm, but to provide some perspective on the risks of being *too entrepreneurial*.

Too opportunistic

It can be hard not to pursue every potential sale or customer opportunity that is presented to you, but successful entrepreneurs build their businesses by remaining focused on their strategic objectives and the action required to achieve them. Time and resources are easily wasted on chasing rainbows if you are not sufficiently selective and don't insist on sticking to the plan.

Both current customers and new prospects will continually present unexpected opportunities. If they are asking for it, you should do it, right? Well, maybe not.

Can you do it well? Profitably? Better than the customer's currently available alternatives?

You don't want everybody to be disappointed at the end of your detour into new territory and you don't want the customers to now conclude that maybe you're not as good as they thought you were.

Your **Go/No-Go decision** on whether or not to pursue any new opportunity should be based on how well it fits with your two most important strategic objectives:

1. **Leveraging your competitive strengths, and**

2. **Building long-term business value.**

Those are the selection criteria that will keep you focused.

Too optimistic

It is important to be optimistic and think positively, but a little paranoia may be wise too. Remember the chairman of Intel, Andy Grove, titled his memoir, *Only the Paranoid Survive*. Mark Zuckerberg has been credited with the same mentality in driving the astonishing growth of Facebook.

Keep a wary eye on the market and monitor your business performance constantly. No news is not good news; you're flying blindfolded. Don't miss or ignore the warning signs of bumpy weather approaching.

Too impatient

Don't expect too much too soon. It seems like everything takes longer than it should and most entrepreneurs have high expectations of themselves and their team. But don't keep changing the plan or trying something new just because you're not there yet. If you're making progress and the end goal is still valid, don't give up too soon.

Too confident

Entrepreneurs usually have great confidence in their instincts and their intelligence. The mistake is to neglect or ignore market feedback and analysis of the facts. Also, being action-oriented, the tendency is to react and 'fire' before the 'ready, aim' stages are complete. Painful surprises can result.

Temper your self-confidence with a little humility – ask for help and get input from others with a stake in the issue before you rush ahead.

Too decisive

Entrepreneurs are expected to be decisive and demonstrate leadership. But both can be overdone – deciding too quickly and providing too much direction, so that employee input, initiative and creativity are stifled.

Often the decision does not need to be made so quickly and the implementation will go more smoothly if time is taken to assess the feedback and answer the questions before commitments are made and the wheels are put in motion.

Back in the 1980's, the Japanese style of management was the primary model for success and one of their recognized tactics was to talk, and talk, and talk about the solution before implementing it.

The result was a much smoother and faster implementation than for the stereotypical decisive American manager, who decides quickly and starts implementation without sufficient prior consultation.

Too creative

Many entrepreneurs are driven to 'Do it my way'; that's why they love running their own business.

But sometimes alternatives have not even been considered and a better way exists. The creative solution may require improvising and learning on the fly, but maybe the best solution is sticking with what works, until it stops working. Or it may be a mistake staying too long with a solution and neglecting to evolve and grow by optimizing systems and processes and installing the best practices and latest technologies available in the industry.

Not everything needs a creative new solution that's unique to you and your business. Maybe you're not that special.

I summarized for the group. "Those were the points I had discussed with Brian and my assessment of the risks of being too entrepreneurial. All of these mistakes can lead to serious difficulties for your business."

Dave added, "It does help to keep in mind that careful analysis and planning are important to offset the tendency to be over-confident, making decisions based on instinct and past experience. I've had to make some quick decisions recently that I'm now going to re-think.

"Even if they were good decisions, I may have come across as arrogant and stubborn. Going ahead in spite of the resistance and objections.

"See you all in a month," he said. "Then we can talk about what changes we've made to avoid being *too entrepreneurial*."

2 > Lead Strategically, Manage Effectively

START WITH A PLAN

As we started our e2eForum, on a bright sunny spring morning, this was on the flipchart:

THE ENTREPRENEUR'S CHALLENGE: STRATEGIC LEADERSHIP + MANAGEMENT EFFECTIVENESS

It's my favourite theme and I had been asked to present today's discussion topic, so there it was. Some of the forum members around the table had heard me rant on this subject before, so I was trying to approach it a little differently this time.

"Today I'm going to start by admitting my own biggest mistake as an entrepreneur – failing to continually think strategically. I was too often pre-occupied with operating issues and short-term problem solving. Stuck in the old dilemma of too busy fighting fires to ever work on fire prevention.

"This was especially true in my first business, computer products distribution. There was so much to learn and so many details to keep on top of – markets and technologies, customer service issues, managing employees and everything I had to know about running a business – from accounting systems and freight rates to bank lines of credit and payroll deductions. I had all the usual excuses for being drawn into the daily crises and never getting back to the drawing board to review our original strategic plan and see if we were still on track.

"To be honest, our original plan was not very strategic and never looked past the first two or three years. It was only focused on making our sales numbers, not on strategic positioning and managing our important business relationships. We made good short-term decisions to maintain profitability and win our share of competitive battles, but we didn't protect ourselves from conflicts with our major suppliers and we weren't prepared for the rapid decline in profit margins as competitors flooded the market.

"We started our business in the mid 1980's, when Apple and IBM personal computers and the clones and compatibles were first landing on desktops in offices, schools and homes everywhere. Initially, our primary product, TTX computer monitors, competed with only about six major brand names and maybe four other regional distributors.

"Our customers were mainly the local computer stores that were on every second street corner and in every shopping centre. We were selling a few hundred monitors a month and average profit margins were at 12% to 14%; pretty healthy we thought. But high profits and fast growth brought a lot of competitors into the market. By the mid 1990's we had over forty competing brand names and at least twenty competing distributors. Profit margins in distribution slid to about 4% – no longer healthy. Our volume was up to three or four thousand monitors a month, more than ten times over our early years, but net profits did not increase and we now had huge risks in inventory and receivables.

"That's when I made the decision to enter into the merger which would have helped us to reduce overhead costs, diversify our product mix and customer portfolio and reduce the risks. Unfortunately, the merger didn't work out and I had to close and re-organize the business before exiting, two years later. Very quickly after that, consolidation eliminated most of the players in personal computer products – leaving only a few major brand names, three large multinational distributors and three or four national retail chains. Any of the survivors from that era had to be very good at re-positioning their businesses to keep up with the rapid evolution of the computer business.

"Your own business may not see such rapid changes in the industry, but whatever business you're in the constantly changing technologies and the innovations from new competitors will continuously affect how you do business. You have to adapt to survive and grow."

Keep your head up

I added, "Don't make the mistake I did of getting lost in the depths of the operating details and neglecting to raise the periscope to scan the horizon for oncoming threats. Keep your head up and be prepared to respond."

"I try to keep aware of what's on the horizon," said Dave, "but sometimes I have very limited choices available for response. We expect our manufacturers to keep up with the competition and our bike dealers to do a good job of attracting customers and making the sale. As a national distributor we provide the pipeline to market, but we need the people at both ends to work with us."

"And it's true," he added, "even if we're in 'old economy' traditional businesses, we all have to keep up with technology – both to remain competitive and to rise to new customer expectations. The technology and the software applications keep getting cheaper, easier to use and more effective at delivering results. We simply cannot afford to stand still – the competition will beat us and the customers will leave us, if we don't keep sharpening our tools."

Looking around the table it seemed we all agreed with Dave. Strategic vision and leadership need to be constantly applied to daily decision making.

Neglecting a strategic focus and failing to provide strategic direction, in my opinion, is the biggest mistake that entrepreneurs make and it can be fatal for their business.

3 → More than the Bottom Line

CREATING BUSINESS VALUE

Most entrepreneurs get into business because they are good at something and want to do more of it, but on their own. Then they discover there are two important management issues that they are not good at – Financial Management and Marketing.

Today's meeting of the e2eForum was going to be focused on financial management and I had suggested the following points for discussion.

Financial Challenges

- **Profit versus Long-term Value**
- **Managing the Balance Sheet**

"Let's start with the same question that I ask my students in the first class on Financial Management, *what is the primary purpose of any business?*"

"Make a profit!"

"Thanks Larry, I was counting on you for the wrong answer. Now let me explain why that's the wrong answer."

I stood in front of the flipchart and emphasized in a few words,

> *"The real purpose of any business is not just to make a profit, it's to create sustainable long-term business value."*

Vivian interjected, "But isn't that just another typical response by big business CEOs defending the obscene profits that are so strongly criticised every day?"

She looked agitated and added, "Please don't tell us, *Greed is good!*"

That pretty much summarized the continuing debate around the profit motive. *Should profit be the primary objective driving decision-making in every business, small and large?*

BEING PROFITABLE IS EASY

I'm not going to defend the excesses of unregulated capitalism or socially irresponsible executives.

I believe very strongly that modern, enlightened capitalists and entrepreneurs will do best for themselves and their companies, their employees, their customers and suppliers, their communities and the planet itself, *if they focus on building long-term business value*.

The right decisions will flow from that focus. A focus on short-term profits will do exactly the opposite.

It's easy to improve short-term profit: reduce maintenance and marketing expenses, neglect product development, cut employee wages and benefits, ignore safety and environmental regulations and avoid taxes; but these actions can all destroy long-term value. Paying attention to those requirements will help to build it.

Good financial management means more than managing the bottom line, whether you're focused on short-term profit or long-term business value. The entrepreneur interested in sustainable and profitable business growth must also manage the Balance Sheet of the business.

The Income Statement shows Profit & Loss and gives insight into the details of revenues and expenses. The Balance Sheet is a presentation of your business assets and liabilities, or in plain English, what you own and what you owe.

Managing your assets is at least as important as managing the bottom line. Failing to monitor and manage your accounts receivable, inventory and cash flow can bring disaster to your business. It's another mistake I'll admit to having made myself.

A $600,000 scuba dive?

We're talking about financial management, but short-term sales management decisions can also lead to value-destroying results. Taking the low margin or high credit-risk order, just to meet the sales revenue targets, can be very bad for your business.

Let me tell you about my own experience with a very scary scuba diving trip. And it wasn't because of the sharks and stingrays.

My daughter started scuba diving while she was at Queen's University and had learned to dive in dirty, cold Lake Ontario. Then she had the bright idea to persuade me to get certified so we could dive together on a trip to the Cayman Islands in the warm clear waters of the Caribbean.

It was spectacular diving on a fascinating variety of coral reef. We were having a great time with two or three dives a day off remote Cayman Brac and staying at a charming little hotel. There was only one phone line in the hotel lobby, which was part of the charm. I was confident that all was well in the capable hands of my management team back at the office anyway. No need to check up on them.

Then one afternoon, walking through the hotel lobby, I heard, "Mr. Chatterson, we have a fax here for you." It was a handwritten note from our technical services manager.

We have a problem with about 400 monitors in Ottawa installed at the federal government. The last delivery seems to be off-spec and the customer wants them all fixed.

Our dealer, Antares, is refusing to pay.

They owe us $600,000.

Suddenly, it was not a good day at the beach.

After a long sleepless night, I decided to call the senior partner at Antares and take an aggressive tone, accusing him of abusing my staff and threatening to ruin my business. He quickly backed off and said, "No, no, no. We just weren't sure how to reach you on vacation and we wanted to get your attention. We can look after it when you're back."

Which we did. But I got a lot more careful about managing my receivables risk. A few years later, when Antares got caught in the industry decline and went into bankruptcy, we only lost about $16,000. Bad, but not enough to kill my business.

That scary scuba diving trip was a sharp warning to start managing credit risk better, while continuing to push sales and keep growing.

KNOW YOUR NUMBERS

"Speaking of financial management, most entrepreneurs are very focused on managing their bottom line by monitoring sales, gross margin and operating expenses. They always know those numbers, right Dave?"

"Yes," Dave said, "but in distribution it's easy. I know my sales results every day and I track profit margins by product line. I know the exact day when I've covered my fixed costs for the month. For the rest of the month, I'm driving profit straight to the bottom line."

"That's good," I said, "but do you know the industry benchmarks for other key performance variables, beyond average gross profit margin? What about sales per sales rep, revenue per square foot of warehouse space or freight cost as a percent of sales. Or the industry average for inventory turnover, working capital ratios and the average number of days in payables or receivables?"

"Jeez, now you're picking on me!?"

"No, Dave, I know you manage your numbers better than most.

But we all need to keep our eye on the scoreboard and monitor our performance against the top performers in our industry and against our own history. It's the only way to be sure that we're staying on track, correcting any deficiencies and making continuous improvements.

"The caution I have for you, is that most business owners neglect asset management, especially cash flow. The business may appear very profitable, but has constant cash flow challenges because management is neglecting control of inventory and receivables, in particular. Unfortunately it is not as simple as the old rule: *Collect fast and Pay slow.* Both customer and supplier relationships can be at risk if cash flow issues force you to be too aggressive in your collections from customers and too lackadaisical in your payments to suppliers.

"Managing the balance sheet also requires good management of your financing to match short-term and long-term needs with short-term and long-term sources of funds. Working with your banker is a very important element of good financial management.

"Let's talk more about that at our next meeting. I'll see you then."

As I rushed out to my morning appointment, I noticed a few pained expressions in the group as they were mentally diving into their own accounts receivable issues.

Relationships are the Key

EMPLOYEES FIRST

Stan was leading the group today and he stood in front of the flipchart which had a blank page covering the discussion points for the meeting. When everyone had settled with their breakfast and their papers on the conference table, he opened the meeting.

"OK, let's start the discussion with a question. Who are the most important people in the success of any business?"

"Customers, of course!" It wasn't just Larry with the obvious answer this time.

"OK," said Stan, "then who can be the biggest obstacle to your success."

"The bank," "Employees," "The government with all their regulations and reporting requirements," "Suppliers, who don't deliver as promised." Now we had some differences of opinion.

So I interjected, "Can we all agree though, that we cannot keep our customers happy and coming back for more, if our employees don't treat them well? And the best way to ensure that happens is to treat our employees the way we would like them to treat our customers."

There was general acknowledgement around the table that employee relationships were key to business success. Stan uncovered the notes on the flipchart that we had prepared for today's agenda.

Key Relationships

- **Employees before customers**
- **Biggest before loudest**
- **Bankers as partners**

I continued, "Isn't it always obvious to the customer when the flight attendant, the service technician or the waitress is not happy with her job? The best lesson I ever got on that subject was actually at a hotel in Las Vegas." *(And it's a story that should not stay in Vegas. So I shared it with the e2eForum.)*

We were at the annual computer conference and exhibition (COMDEX) in Las Vegas and my partners and I were having a long breakfast meeting in the Treasure Island Casino dining room. Long after breakfast we were still getting smiling and prompt service from the waiter with never-ending cups of coffee. We were there for so long that the shift changed, but we still had friendly, attentive service from the waitress who was now bringing the refills.

Finally, after we had remarked on the good service among ourselves, I said to her, 'We've been coming to this conference in Vegas for years and we've met in many different dining rooms, but this is absolutely the best service we've ever had. How do you do it?"

She said, "It's because of the owner, Steve Wynn. He treats us so well, we treat everybody well in return."

Ba-da-boom. She got it. And the message stuck for me.

"Great story, Uncle Ralph, and I agree," said Brian, "but what if that well-treated employee still just doesn't get it."

"That happens, for sure." I said. "I remember a service technician telling me that his sharing in the monthly sales bonus made no difference to him; he still treated all the customers like idiots. Apparently we had made a hiring decision that was a mistake. So we asked him to leave and take his bad attitude elsewhere.

"Recognizing and removing the misfits is a difficult but necessary part of people management. If employees do not buy into the corporate culture, they will never be effective members of the team and they need to be removed. Doing it well is important, though, because all of your employees are watching the departure and judging you as a manager by how you handle it.

"When I was doing a survey to develop my list of the Seven Biggest Mistakes that Entrepreneurs Make, one entrepreneur suggested it should include, *Hiring too fast and firing too slow*. He had a good point and it reminded me of the time I made both mistakes with the same employee!

"And I know you want to hear that story, right?"

"Sure," said Larry, "I find it reassuring to know you made so many mistakes and still survived!"

"Well, let's just remember the old cliché, 'What doesn't kill you makes you stronger.' Or as Bill Gates used to say at Microsoft, 'In this business you have to recognize your mistakes quickly, before they get big enough to kill you.'

"Most of the time I did fail fast and move on, but my merger was a big mistake and it did kill my business because I didn't reverse the decision fast enough.

"Fortunately, I 'survived' because I had a good network of business associates, employees and customers, as well as enough cash on the side, to re-start. That's something else you need to do. Make sure you can survive the failure of your business by taking out enough cash during the good years for yourself and your family. Build that *Basic Defensive Interval* again for next time.

"But back to Bob (not his real name, of course), and my mistake of hiring him too fast and firing him too slow. He was a sales rep with a bit of a mixed track record and some contradictory references –

'great guy, good results, but hard to manage.' Of course, I thought I was a better manager than his previous bosses and I needed a sales rep, so we signed him up. He did well for a few months, bringing some new customers with him and quickly getting some big orders for us. But he was hard to keep track of and I started to notice his work habits were letting us down. Late for meetings or not showing up at all; refusing to make the extra effort if it interfered with his personal agenda.

"So after about a year, one more refusal to go out of his way for a customer caused me to sit him down and *counsel him out*. (That was the clumsy euphemism we used at Coopers and Lybrand Management Consultants to advise someone that their career plan would be better served somewhere else. Instead of delivering the very clear message, *you're fired!*) Then I compounded the error with Bob by trying to be kind and giving him some referrals to other companies that might be hiring. That wasn't doing him or his next employer any favours. I should have been more frank about his deficiencies with both of them.

"Immediately after Bob had left us, I started to learn from employees and customers that he was an even bigger problem than I thought; not only were his working relationships contentious with everyone, but he also had another business on the side that he was working at with his wife when he was supposed to be working for us. 'What took you so long to let him go?' was a comment I heard too often.

"So in terms of hiring, firing and managing performance, I learned to include other managers in the process and to be much more observant of who the team players are and who are not. Who get it and who do not. To recognize good or bad performance and to encourage feedback. My guiding principle remains: *Praise in public; Punish in private.* But it's never quite that simple.

"Dealing with poor performance is only one of the challenges in managing employee relationships. Recognizing and rewarding high performance employees is also a very important priority, even if they need less supervision and micro-management. They need to be engaged and developed to meet their goals. Help them to act as if they're owners too – always working to promote the company and to improve its performance. Mismanaging your top performers puts at risk one of the most important relationships for building value in your business."

WHO'S SQUEAKING NOW?

"But back to the all-important customer relationship," said Vivian. "Don't the same principles apply to managing good and bad customers? I find it's easy to make the mistake of being distracted by the most annoying and persistent customers and neglecting the biggest and best, who are not likely to be the 'squeakiest,' just the most important. They're easy to forget about because they require less service and support, but it's a big mistake to neglect them. Not only do they bring important revenue to the business, they also influence a lot of other customers. They deserve VIP treatment."

"That's right, Vivian," said Dave. "But don't forget you may also have to squeak more yourself. Do your suppliers appreciate you enough? Maybe you're more important to them than you realize. For example, you may discover that they love you for always paying so promptly and you can get preferential pricing or terms, if you just ask. I know it can make a big difference if you push your suppliers to do better for you."

He added, "My most important supplier is actually my bank and unfortunately they're just not keeping up with my rapid sales growth. We started with a line of credit of $50,000 at RBC Bank, supported by personal guarantees and secured by our inventory and our receivables with the bike shops. But sales are growing so fast the bank calls it 'over-trading,' which means they're not comfortable with the rapid increases that have brought the credit limit up to $750,000. They will not go to $1,000,000 in spite of the good history and the solid security because according to the credit manager, 'we're at the limit for consumer products in our branch portfolio.' That's not helping me, so I'm going to the BMoC Bank who have been aggressively seeking our business for a while now and they like our financials. They're willing to give me everything I want – a higher credit limit, lower interest rate, reduced personal guarantees and a few other goodies like better foreign exchange rates and free electronic funds transfers. I'm signing with them next week. Believe me; it pays to build a good credit rating and maintain a good banking relationship."

"Thanks, Dave," I said. "That's a very relevant example of managing your banking relationship. It's a good introduction to this article that I wrote a few years ago for my Blog at LearningEntrepreneurship.com."

I started to hand-out the article that I had planned to circulate today.

IS YOUR BANK A WELCOME AND WILLING PARTNER IN YOUR BUSINESS?

Many business owners do not consider their bankers as welcome and willing partners in their business. Yet it is an important relationship that will often affect your ability to grow and to survive periods of financial stress. You want to treat your banker like your best customer, not your worst supplier.

Working with an unwilling and unwelcome partner is obviously not a very constructive relationship. A more effective partnership with your banker can be built on some of the following assumptions:

1. They will not get it.

Start by accepting that your bankers will never fully understand what you do for a living – your motivation, your challenges or your circumstances. But you do have to try to get them to understand enough about you and your business operations so that they can be confident that working with you will be good for them.

Remember the bank's primary role is <u>not</u> to lend you money; it's to earn a return on their investment for their shareholders and limit the risk of losing any money.

2. It's only for the money.

You will need to prove that the money is all you need; because you have already looked after everything else.

The banker does not want to worry about your customers, your management team, your sales and marketing efforts, your operating efficiencies, your health, your marriage or anything else except the financial services you need.

3. They have a checklist.

When you meet and fill in the forms, remember the banker wants to be satisfied on these five criteria:

- **Character** – do you have a reputation of integrity and responsibility on your prior financial obligations?

- **Capital** – do you have enough invested in your business to be personally at risk?

- **Capacity** – will you be able to support the cash flow requirements of any new loans?

- **Collateral** – if you ever fail to repay your loans, what assets are available to the bank to recover them?

- **Conditions** – is your industry currently in good economic condition with potential for growth or is it heading for a downturn?

  Good answers for the bank on these points will provide the start to a good relationship with a confident and willing partner instead of tentative support from a cautious and reluctant partner.

4. Reduce the risk.

You may be stimulated by risk and reward; your banker is not.

Banking is a very conservative career choice. Regardless of how good you and your plans are, the banker will still want personal guarantees. That means he gets your house if you fail.

(Personal Note: I've never met a banker who found it amusing to suggest that you should get his house if you succeed.)

5. Think big.

The more you need, the more interested they'll be and you'll likely get better terms. (The only time I had no personal guarantees was when our loans were at $4.8 million. My puny personal guarantee would have made no difference, they had to bet on the company.) So, if you're starting small, be sure to describe your growth plans and your intention to build a strong, long-term relationship with *this* bank.

6. Get a second opinion.

Bankers love to win business away from other banks. That's good for their career plans. (That's how we got the $4.8 million with favourable terms.) So check out the competition anytime you need new financing or your current bank is not serving you well. Just be sincere and be ready to change.

One banker asked me directly, "If I meet all your requests will you move your accounts to my bank?" I said, "Yes."

He delivered and so did we.

7. It's not a people business.

It's a numbers business and you cannot negotiate with a computer. That friendly, helpful person you're talking to does not make the decisions.

Your numbers will get fed into some obscure computer program and the answers (or more questions) will pop out. They are not negotiable. A good banking relationship means that your account manager will tell you what numbers are required from you to get more favourable answers.

8. Manage your numbers

Make sure your business plan computes and gives financial results that are attractive to lenders. (Remember, *pure fiction* is not allowed.) Then manage the numbers to deliver the results and stay within the limits set by the bank.

Read the fine print to be sure you understand any restrictions on use of the funds and you don't miss any requirements to maintain certain financial ratios. Deliver financial reports as required, but also be sure to provide your own analysis and explanations to your account manager before someone else does. You don't want their computers to set off any alarms.

9. No surprises, please.

Bad news is never well received, but the reaction will be much worse if it's also a surprise. And no news at all only makes them worry.

Keep your banker aware of what might go wrong and what you plan to do about it. Then keep them current as things evolve, so they get used to your ever-changing circumstances and how you're handling them. (Hopefully, well.)

Avoid going back with a new plan too soon or too often. And try to plan well ahead of any request for more financing. It is very hard to get the bank to help you out of a disaster when you're in it.

10. People still matter.

The personal connection is still a very important part of a good relationship with your bank. Part of managing that relationship is to be sure that you are not entirely dependent on just one contact. If the relationship lasts, your contact person will change and you need to know someone else to maintain continuity of the relationship. Stay connected at several levels.

Your banking relationship needs to be strong to withstand the inevitable hard times that hit any business. A welcome and willing partner should help you weather those occasional storms.

It was an old article, but it still seemed to strike a chord as everyone slipped it into their notebooks, exchanging more stories of unsupportive bankers, as they left the meeting.

Marketing is NOT Everything

IT'S A THREE-PART PROCESS

Today's discussion was being led by Dave, who considered marketing to be his biggest strength and the key to his rapid success in growing sales for his bicycle distribution business.

He started with the comment, "Marketing is not everything. But it is the first important step in a three-part process to deliver satisfied customers who keep coming back for more. So these are the key points for discussion today."

Building your Business

- Goal = Long-term, loyal, profitable customers.
- Process = Marketing + Sales + Customer Service

"Who wants to start?"

"Let me add," I said, "that marketing is an area that entrepreneurs often either neglect or do badly. Marketing is kind of like the restaurant business; we're all exposed to it enough that we think we understand how it works.

"I want to emphasize Dave's two key points on the flipchart: the goal and the process."

BUILDING LOYAL, LONG-TERM, PROFITABLE CUSTOMERS

Goal:

All efforts must be dedicated to the primary objective of every business: building loyal, long-term, profitable customer relationships.

Process:

It's a three-part process: Marketing + Sales + Customer Service.

"It's all about finding, attracting and retaining customers that bring value to the business in continuous profitable revenue and also become our biggest fans, telling everybody how wonderful we are. Sometimes we get so preoccupied with the hard work managing our marketing and sales efforts we forget that essential strategic objective.

"The financial objective, of course, is to generate and grow sales revenue and profits. But to have sales you need customers. And to have sustained, profitable and growing sales, the best strategy is to develop loyal, long-term customer relationships.

"So the marketing, sales and customer service activities must all be aligned to deliver a customer experience with your company and your brand that evolves from a first time buyer to a long-term customer. The marketing and sales efforts bring in the first order and then customer service has to deliver on the rest."

The **customer experience** with any business should evolve through four levels:

1. **Satisfaction with price and availability**
   On the first exposure to your business, customers will quickly, maybe even subconsciously, compare price and availability to their expectations based on prior experience with your competition. If this minimum expectation is not met, there will likely be no sale and maybe no second chance.

2. **Recognition of superior service levels**
   The first point of differentiation and the first step to building a stronger customer relationship will be when the customer recognizes that you offer superior service. You can demonstrate it in many ways – more stock, better delivery, easier payment

terms, faster response to inquiries or better customer service and support. Any one of these may be sufficient for you to stand out from the competition and deliver a satisfied customer.

3. **Appreciation of the value of your knowledge and experience**
   After the basic needs of price and availability are met and you have distinguished yourself with superior service, the customer experience should then lead to an appreciation of the added value of your knowledge and experience. This will be demonstrated by your staff having the product knowledge, training, education and experience to help customers make better purchasing decisions. Now you're building a relationship valued by the customer.

4. **Connection on values, mission and vision**
   The final step in cementing loyal, long-term relationships will occur when the customer recognizes a common sense of values, mission and vision in the way you do business. This connection will be developed over several interactions, particularly when problems are solved together, or you connect on issues not directly related to the buy-sell transaction like honesty and integrity, social responsibility or environmental issues.

"The sooner you can meet customer expectations at all four levels, the faster you will build lasting and loyal customer relationships. And that is the primary objective of every business, right? Does anybody think 'buy and goodbye' is a business model that works for anybody?"

Vivian had an answer, "Well, if you're selling kitchen appliances, it might be ten or fifteen years before the customer needs another one."

"Also true for high performance bikes," said Dave. "They may make only one big purchase every six or seven years. And that's why bike shops try to add accessories to their product line – helmets, shoes and clothing – as well as keep in touch with the customers for service and tune-ups. Most have a Website and Blog or Twitter account or an e-newsletter to build brand loyalty through the levels three and four that Uncle Ralph mentioned – demonstrating the added-value of their knowledge and experience as well as confirming common values and vision around cycling."

"I realize we do that too in combining our pet store with the vet clinic," said Vivian. "They are very complementary services and products, always sharing the love for animals. We already have customers who've lasted longer than their pets!"

Brian raised his hand to interrupt, "These are all good concepts, but what about all the little things we need to do? I have a technology business that is immersed in the digital side of business and all our marketing, sales and customer support services are done online with Web marketing and e-commerce applications, but I think some of the traditional methods still apply to build strong customer loyalty."

"You're right, Brian," I said and started making more notes on the flipchart.

MARKETING, SALES OR CUSTOMER SERVICE?

Do we need to deliver on all three?

"First, let's clearly define each of the three elements of this process to build long-term valuable customer relationships."

1. **Marketing** – understanding the market and defining the target customer; building awareness, interest, and attraction; and identifying prospects.

2. **Sales** – converting interested prospects into qualified, buying customers.

3. **Customer service** – delivering products and services as promised to ensure that each customer is a satisfied, repeat customer.

"Each step has to be done consistently well for the results to be achieved. But a choice still has to be made - which element are you going to be best at? Will you win from competitors on marketing, sales, or customer service? You cannot be *best* at all three.

"In my experience, managing a second-tier brand name in computer hardware, we knew that we couldn't possibly out-market the multinationals, but we could out-sell them – one customer at a time. We spent a minimum of time and effort on marketing. Respecting basic principles of clear and consistent messaging and being creative at avoiding large expenditures. That worked for us.

"Winning on customer service was also a challenge – it's expensive for any manufacturer to compete on warranty terms and technical support. So we went back to salesmanship, even in the service department – coaching staff on persuading the customer to be reasonable and patient and give us another chance, *please!* We carefully explained to all our service technicians that the best result from a call for technical support was to turn a complaint into a compliment and then pass the call to a sales rep for another order.

"You can best achieve success by being selective, instead of trying to be good at everything. So take a look at your strategic positioning, your performance and your options in marketing, sales and customer service - then choose, focus and build one of them into your competitive weapon."

THE SIX P'S OF MARKETING

"Now Dave, you did ask for a checklist and I have one prepared for today," I said, as I passed copies around the table.

"You've probably heard of the Four P's of Marketing. Well, I've revised and expanded them up to six. No extra charge. Build your marketing objectives and plan around these six P's of Marketing – three strategic and three operational. Here's the checklist."

The Six P's of Marketing

STRATEGIC:

1. **Positioning:**
   - Strategic positioning of the product relative to competitors in the target market sector will affect all the other elements – placement, promotion, product, pricing, and packaging.
   - Choice of high versus low in quality, price, and service.

2. **Placement:**
   - Where is the product or service to be made available for customers?
   - Choices of retail or wholesale, online or storefront, direct sale or through distributors and sales agents.

3. **Promotion:**
   - Choices of priorities, budget and effort.
   - Direct marketing, advertising.
   - Public relations activities, participation in industry associations, conferences, trade shows.
   - Website, search engine optimisation and web marketing programs.
   - Promotional items, sponsorships.

OPERATIONAL:

4. **Products:**
   - Development of the product or service.
   - Features and benefits offered relative to competitors.
   - Plans to meet changing market demands.

5. **Pricing:**
   - Determined by the market and target sector, competition and customer expectations.

- Price relative to cost to determine profit margins.
- Volume discounts, incentives or variable pricing.

6. **Packaging:**
   - Choices of style, colours and packaging consistent with corporate image and identity.
   - Warranty, service, accessories included.
   - Regulatory requirements.
   - Retail display choices, shipping & handling issues.

"And that's pretty much the one page course in Marketing and Product Management, which is all we have time for today, since we haven't talked about Sales Management yet."

"How do we know if that's a problem?" asked Larry.

"It's always a problem," said Paul.

"Only if you neglect it," said Dave.

I added, "You know there's a problem brewing when you hear an entrepreneur explaining that, 'The product sells itself,' or 'Price is all that matters,' or 'Our sales reps need to do a better job.' Those complaints are all signs that the company is failing at both marketing and sales management.

"Not only are opportunities for profitable growth being missed, but the company may be on the downward slide to out of business without a well-conceived and sustained marketing plan and effective sales management."

I went back to the flipchart, "Here's my simple approach to Sales Management and four more P's!"

But first, let me suggest some simple **Guiding Principles for Sales Management**

- **Sales objective** is to make targeted prospects into active customers.
- **Sales process** is to take leads from marketing, qualify them as interested prospects, make the sales pitch and get the order.
- **Sales rep** needs to be known, liked, respected and trusted, in that order, for sales success.
- **Remind the rep**: Sell yourself first, then the company, then the product.

"It is, of course more difficult and complicated than that, but for basic Sales Management, these guiding principles will get you a long way."

THE FOUR P'S OF SALESMANSHIP

Patient, Persistent, Polite and Persuasive

"OK, now I have to tell you my favourite story on salesmanship. Not an original and probably not even true, but very instructive anyway." They looked a little concerned, but I continued.

A high-powered IBM executive working in New York used to take the subway to the office every day and he noticed there was a young man always positioned at the top of the stairs to the street with a box of books at his feet and two or three books in his hands, politely asking every passerby, "You wanna buy a book?"

He was there rain or shine, hot or cold, every morning and evening as hundreds of commuters passed by. After several months of observing this hard-working, polite but persistent, casually dressed, but personable young man asking everyone who passed, "You wanna buy a book?" the IBM executive stopped one morning to speak to him.

He said, "Young man, I'm very impressed with you working so hard selling books here every day and I'd like to offer you a job at IBM. We can get you started in our sales training program right away and within a year or two you could be making $60,000 to $80,000 a year."

The young man politely replied, 'Why thank you very much, sir, but I'm already doing better than that. You wanna buy a book?"

Dave laughed out loud, as others smiled, and he said, "I'm definitely telling that story to one of my reps who is trying too hard and making it too complicated. He's reading books, going to courses, sitting in on Webinars, following the experts on Blogs and so on, but he gets so caught up in the process that he neglects to just ask the question, 'You wanna buy some bikes?' It drives me crazy sometimes listening to him on long distance to Vancouver or San Francisco. He rambles on about the weather and the football and the economy before he finally asks about their inventory and gets to the point, 'Do you need some bikes?' In fact I'm putting this on the agenda for our next sales meeting: *Keep it simple and ask for the order.*"

That got such a good response I couldn't resist another sales story. I started with a short preamble.

"A suggestion I often have for sales managers is to recognize their top sales reps and get them involved in sharing their tactics with the other reps. Learn from the best. It's also a good way to build the sales team by sharing ideas and information, like we do here. If it doesn't go well, it may be a warning sign that your sales compensation plan is promoting competition and jealousy instead of co-operation and teamwork.

"So I have another story to help you remember that principle of sales management. I probably should give credit to the great Zig Ziglar for these stories, but I honestly don't remember where I heard them first. I've just been repeating them for years."

This story is about a company selling safety glass that had a direct sales force calling on customers all over the U.S. Each year they had a sales conference where they celebrated their successes and recognized the top achievers. For several years, old Charlie had won the top sales award, so one year they asked him what he did to win so many orders.

He was willing to share and explained, "When I finally get an appointment, I sit down with the buyer and I bring out the samples of our safety glass to compare to the samples of our competitors. Then I bring out my hammer and I smash them all right there on the conference table! Now I have their attention to make my pitch."

Well that year a lot of sales reps went out with their samples and their hammers. But again Charlie won the top sales award. So again the VP of Sales asked Charlie, in front of a large audience, "What did you do differently this year?"

Charlie said, "I gave the hammer to the buyer."

That story too got a good response, but it was time to conclude the discussion on sales management. "Enough checklists and bad stories to take away for today," I said. "Just remember the secret formula is simple: *Sell like hell!* Never quit selling. Get your team focused on the one thing that solves all your problems – more sales."

GOOD CUSTOMER SERVICE IS SIMPLE, NOT EASY

"Now we've talked about getting the customer's attention through effective marketing and getting the order through good salesmanship, but what about the final step to deliver a satisfied repeat customer – exceptional customer service?"

There were a few sheepish looks around the table, but Vivian spoke up, "I think that's what we do best. We suck at marketing and sales, because we're all so respectful of the customer that we're reluctant to appear at all pushy. Our style is very much in line with our whole approach to the business –*How can we help you take better care of your pet?*"

"Sounds exactly right," said Dave. "Your staff are immediately aligned with the customer at the top level of vision and values. You can probably still work on the marketing to get people into the store and salesmanship to get the staff to push for more sales, but you're already doing well at attracting and retaining loyal customers."

"I agree," added Brian, "it's the best way to close a sale; demonstrate your interest in the customer's problem before you present your solution. Listen before you start selling. Remember the old consulting mantra: *They don't care what you know until they know that you care.* It works for us."

I added, "I've noticed, though, that when entrepreneurs are trying to understand their customer's needs, they often mistakenly assume that they think like a customer. But that's not always the case. It may be true for Vivian as a conscientious pet owner, but most of us have to do market research and customer surveys to keep up with our customers and their changing needs and expectations, as well as listen very carefully to what they're telling us.

"It's not always easy to do, as the customer is not always right and often has totally unreasonable expectations. But it's a good simple rule. Listen to what the customer wants and then find a way to deliver it. As customers ourselves, the last thing we want to hear from customer service after we make our request to solve a problem is, *'I'm sorry, but company policy doesn't allow us to do that.'*

"Maybe the first rule for customer service should be to make sure everyone knows how far they can go in breaking the rules. We all love to hear that attentive, helpful customer service rep tell us that she can fix our billing problem and also reduce our billing by $12 a month. It might be a simple fix that removes the sting of getting ripped off for the previous many months.

"The important point about customer service is the one that we made earlier talking about key relationships."

Employees need to be treated well if we expect them to treat the customers well.

We had covered a lot of ground on marketing, sales and customer service (not to mention too many anecdotes) and we were well past the regular 9:00AM deadline. So we agreed to postpone the Members' Wrap-up Roundtable and conclude this meeting of the e2eForum.

Let's do it Again

MAYBE THE FIRST TIME IS YOUR ONLY TIME

We all tried hard to arrive early for the e2eForum meetings because it gave us time to chat informally with the other members and exchange comments on our businesses and other issues that were not on the day's agenda.

Unfortunately, an accident on the expressway this morning had kept me from arriving early enough to review the agenda with Stan, who was chairing the meeting this week, and he had already set up the flipchart.

Serial Entrepreneurship

- **Another Start-up?**
- **Or the next Screw- up?**

What I heard on arrival was Paul talking to Dave. "It looks like a safe bet. My son has some experience in the restaurant business. I've got the initial $160,000 and financing is easy for the rest of the investment because banks love franchises."

Paul was talking about the gourmet hamburger franchise he was considering investing in with his son.

"Sorry, Paul," said Dave, "but experience flipping burgers doesn't mean your son knows how to run a burger joint. Even if the franchisor delivers all the management tools and support, do you really want to get involved in that business? Every day you'll have to manage minimum wage staff and deal with unhappy customers complaining that your burgers suck. All your experience has been managing highly qualified machinists and selling precision parts to major multinational manufacturing businesses."

"Yes, and I built a successful business in that industry," said Paul. "This should be much easier. I have the time and the money and I need a new challenge to keep from getting bored. I don't want to spend every day in retirement watching my money ride the stock market roller coaster."

"It sounds like your entrepreneurial juices are still percolating, Paul," I said. "But maybe you should go back to the start-up criteria we talked about a few months ago. Look for an opportunity that really leverages your unique skills, knowledge, experience and contacts. Isn't that what worked for you the first time?"

"True enough. All I bring to this business is a long history of eating hamburgers!" Paul was laughing at himself now and it looked like he would leave his money in the bank – for a while.

I was remembering what I've said many times to other successful businessmen: *Making money doesn't make you smart.*

What I said out loud to the group was, "Before you throw your energy and money into a new venture, ask yourself a few important questions."

"I hear another checklist coming!" chirped Larry.

"Thanks Larry, now I'll have to give it a name. Let's call it the **Encore Performance Checklist.**"

"If you're determined to boast that you're a serial entrepreneur, not just a successful entrepreneur; then ask yourself these questions before you get started on your next venture:

- What was it that made you succeed in your first business? Did you build your business on your unique knowledge or ability, a new product idea, a preferred customer or supplier relationship? Which of these will apply to the new business?

- What mistakes have you avoided in the past? Are you about to make those mistakes now?

- What new risks are you encountering for the first time?

- Is now a good time to start something new? Are there no challenges left in your current business?

- How much will a new initiative impact your current business and the demands on your time and resources?

- Is your past success really transferable to the new business?

"Many successful entrepreneurs have made the mistake of jumping into a new venture – merger, acquisition, restaurant franchise or real estate investment – and blown away the equity value they built in their original business. It's another costly mistake to avoid."

Brian shared his own conclusion with us, "I'm now convinced that the next venture is something to set aside until I'm at the exit stage like Paul. When my current business is running itself and I have the time and money to *very carefully* select the next opportunity. I just don't want to wait until I'm that old, sorry Paul. I'm thinking I'll be ready for my next business adventure at thirty-five."

Stan added, "Too late for me, I'm already thirty-nine, but I'd like to accelerate the plan to get to that stage soon too. Then I can start the next business before I get bored and screw up the one I've got."

I said, "I've seen that happen a few times. Entrepreneurs who started to dabble in something more exciting, thinking their business was on cruise control and they could let it go. It headed into a crash landing instead. So let's avoid the unhappy ending of an exit by default. Put it on the agenda for a future meeting – *Preparing for Exit.*"

We all agreed that was a good topic for a future meeting and concluded the e2eForum with our regular Roundtable Wrap-up and an update from each of the members before heading out for the day.

Let's get Personal

I AM NOT YOUR MOTHER

The discussion had already started when I arrived and I heard Paul saying with a laugh, "OK, OK. I've given up on the hamburger business."

"Glad we helped you avoid that misadventure," I said.

Today we had agreed to talk about personal issues that affect the business, particularly issues involving family in the business.

This was on the flipchart:

Personal Issues

- **Family in or out?**
- **Employees like family?**

Paul started the discussion by reminding us of his own story.

"I've had some bad experiences with relatives interfering in my business, but mixing family and business isn't all bad. My wife has been a tremendous help at critical times over the years and both my son and daughter pitched in during the early years to do some of the grunt work. It was good for them, too. Exposed them to business from the inside and probably helped persuade them to head for university and get into a good profession, instead of running a business like me!"

"Maybe I should have taken that route instead of taking over my dad's business," said Stan. "But for me it was different. I started working summers with my dad, but then after high school I thought I wanted to do something else, so I went to work with a big construction company. After a while, I realized I was happier to be in a small family business and returned to work with my dad. I appreciated the satisfaction that comes with being close to senior management and being recognized for contributing to the success of the business."

"That pretty much sums up the challenges," I said. "How do you include family members that are interested and capable and still give employees who are not part of the family the same level of satisfaction? Can you make them feel they are valued as effective members of the team without being members of the family? That they still might be the boss, someday? How can you treat them like part of the family without confusing the boundaries between boss and employee? Can you even be friends with your employees?"

Dave said, "That was about the first lesson I learned as a young engineer after getting promoted to production supervisor. Within a few months or so I had to suspend a friend for three days without pay for a safety violation; in spite of the fact that I had spent the weekend water-skiing with him. It was tough to remain friends after that."

"It's a choice of management style," I said. "I've seen them all – from rough use-and-abuse them managers to the paternalistic godfather who insists on getting involved in the personal lives of all his employees. The abusive, controlling style is dysfunctional because it requires micro-management of every detail and creates an environment where employees just try to stay out of trouble and avoid mistakes.

"But the paternalistic style goes too far in the other direction, I think. It creates a sense of complacency, relieves employees of their sense of responsibility and reduces their willingness to take initiative and make decisions.

"My preference is a management style that is respectful and kind, but encourages employees to think and act like part-owners of the business. Encouraging a sense of responsibility and a willingness to make decisions and take initiative, even if it means accepting mistakes and their consequences. That style also makes it easier to manage the business and to eventually exit, as the business becomes much less dependent on the owner."

Distracted by Personal Issues

"Unfortunately, you can still be distracted by personalities and personal issues that may seriously affect business performance. The distracting personality may be an owner, manager or employee and it can be a mistake if the issues are simply ignored until they become a problem.

"The problems may be a clash of personalities affecting working relationships and they have to be dealt with one-on-one by the manager. Sometimes the problems come from the top performers that get carried away and start behaving like rock stars."

BUSINESS OR FAMILY?

"Family businesses have particular issues to navigate," added Dave, "My kids also worked in the business during the summers and it was a challenge. My daughter was very uncomfortable as the boss's daughter. My son managed to fit better as an employee and even started calling me Dave at work, instead of Dad. Maybe that was the secret."

"Yes," I said, "family members in the business add new challenges. On the other hand, as Stan's father told him, family members can usually be trusted more than outsiders to take care of the business.

"Sometimes, however, that can be a problem too. I was invited at one time to help a business owner whose daughter was the office manager. Unfortunately, she was protective of his interests to the point of being paranoid and obsessive about managing every detail. She was so aggressive and tactless with employees that one receptionist we hired actually quit before noon the first day because of her. I eventually persuaded the owner that both his business and his daughter would benefit if she made career plans elsewhere.

"Even if your family is not in the business, they can still have a powerful influence, especially your parents. I don't know about you, but I'm still trying to impress my mother and follow the advice of my father."

LISTEN TO MOM

"Yeah, that never ends," said Stan, "even after they're gone."

"You're right," I said. "My mother once told me, 'Don't do anything that you wouldn't do if I were there.' That got my attention. It was a great way to keep me on the straight and narrow as a teenager, but I still imagine her checking up on me every day.

"Worth keeping in mind as entrepreneurs. Mothers are an important influence on our ethical conduct in business. I like the way it was stated by a small-town jeweler, who had a conspicuous sign posted next to the cash register stating, 'We give instant credit to all our customers. If they're over ninety and accompanied by their mother.' A great credit guideline!

"Most entrepreneurs and executives probably don't often think about their mothers on the job – unless she's the boss, like Ma Boyle at Columbia Sportswear. Maybe they should. We'd probably have fewer issues of corporate misconduct, if the executives' mothers knew what was going on. Perhaps instead of all those business management courses and books on ethics and corporate social responsibility, we only need to remind decision-makers, "Would your mother be proud of you, if she knew what you were doing?"

"As your Uncle Ralph, I'm still inspired by my father's unique character and wise advice and my mother had a strong influence on my management style, although she was more subtle. It was less frequently stated than demonstrated. Quiet, hardworking and good humoured, responsible and respectful of others; those are the characteristics that immediately come to mind. Things we all learned from her example. Of course, she was also good at reminding us when we forgot those important principles or our behaviour was not up to her standards. And it's still a pleasure to make her proud.

"That's why I recommend you use the test 'What would Mom think?' before making difficult ethical decisions in your business."

But I am not your mother

Now I'm suggesting that we might have better decision-making if we asked ourselves what Mom would think. But what about those employees who expect you to act like their mother?

What's the right level of caring and compassion before it becomes more personal than a working relationship should be? Is there a reasonable limit? Is it appropriate to get involved with issues that are strictly personal? Do employees become part of your extended family with all the additional obligations that implies?

Some recent exposure to business owners dealing with their employees' personal issues has caused me to become more cautious. Once managers start offering a sympathetic ear and then a shoulder to cry on, it soon becomes more time-consuming on and off the job and creates a relationship that is difficult to steer back to business only. It also becomes a distraction for other employees and creates new concerns about employee favouritism.

My guideline for these situations would be to decide whether you would, or should, do what is being requested for every employee in the same situation. Offer financial advice or a cash advance? Special working hours or more time off? Bring the kids or the dog to the office? If you would rather not, then say no to the first request. Don't start a precedent that you're not prepared to offer to everyone and write into your corporate policy manual. You do have a policy manual, right?

Don't be afraid to clarify the relationship. "I'm your boss, not your mother. This is a business, not a social safety net."

The members at the e2eForum looked slightly uncomfortable with communicating that message, but the meeting came to a close. We were all reflecting on the role of family in our businesses.

The Seven Biggest Mistakes and How to Avoid Them

In the preceding chapters we have worked our way through what I call the **Entrepreneur's Challenge**, providing strategic leadership and delivering effective business management.

Once you have your business started, the real challenge will be to successfully keep it growing and profitable. There will be many opportunities to make mistakes and to stumble into unexpected problems.

From my experience, confirmed by most entrepreneurs, it is normal and acceptable to make mistakes as long as they are small and recognized early. You will fail occasionally. It's all part of the learning experience to get better and do better.

But there are some big mistakes that can kill your business.

THE LIST

I've developed a list of the **Seven Biggest Mistakes that Entrepreneurs Make**. You will notice that we have covered all seven of them through our discussions in the e2eForum, described in the preceding seven chapters.

Following is a re-cap for your review and future reference with my recommendations on how to avoid them.

#1 Too Entrepreneurial

Certain characteristics of entrepreneurs are necessary for them to be successful. But if over-indulged they can lead to big mistakes. These include the tendency to be too opportunistic and not sufficiently selective and focused; to be too optimistic and miss or ignore the warning signs; to be too impatient and expect too much too soon.

Entrepreneurs usually have great confidence in their instincts, but the mistake is to neglect or ignore market feedback and analysis of the facts. Being action-oriented, the tendency is to "just do it".

Entrepreneurs are expected to be decisive and demonstrate leadership, but both can be overdone – deciding too quickly and providing too much direction so that input, initiative and creativity are stifled.

These mistakes can arise from being *too entrepreneurial*.

#2 Lack of Strategic Direction

Another tendency of many entrepreneurs is to get lost in the daily details and completely neglect their original strategic objectives and plan.

Operating decisions demand continuous attention and there is seldom time dedicated to stepping back and looking at the business from a strategic perspective. The common observation is that the owner is too busy working *in* his business to effectively work *on* his business.

Defaulting to continuous short-term decision-making can result in the business not having consistent strategic direction and straying far away from the original plan.

Lack of strategic direction may be the single biggest mistake that entrepreneurs make.

#3 Focused on Profit

Being focused on profit doesn't seem like a mistake. After all, isn't that the whole purpose of running a business? No, actually. As we discussed, the primary financial objective of any business is *to enhance long-term business value*.

Many short-term profit-oriented decisions can hurt long-term value. Most entrepreneurs are very focused on managing the bottom line by monitoring sales, gross margin and expenses. They always know those numbers. But they too often neglect asset management, especially cash flow.

Managers need to look at all their key performance variables and react quickly to avoid big mistakes.

#4 Neglecting Key Relationships

The key relationship for any business is the one between management and staff. Good communications are essential to providing strategic leadership and ensuring that management and staff are working effectively as a team toward common goals.

Sometimes we are distracted from our key relationships by the most annoying and challenging employee or customer. Often your biggest customers are not the *squeakiest*, just the most important. And do you need to squeak more yourself? Do your suppliers appreciate you enough?

Another important relationship is with your banker. *Is your bank a welcome and willing partner in your business?*

Building and protecting these key relationships are essential steps to keeping your business on track and meeting your strategic objectives.

#5 Poor Marketing and Sales Management

There are usually obvious signs of poor marketing and sales management. Feedback from customers may also highlight your failures in customer service. Opportunities for growth are being missed and current customers are fading away.

No business can survive without effective marketing and sales management supported by consistent customer service. All three functions need to be done well to build loyal, long-term profitable customer relationships.

#6 "That was Easy, Let's Do It Again!"

Another common mistake that can have devastating consequences on the business is the over-confident entrepreneur who concludes, "That was easy, let's do it again!" So he or she jumps into new markets, new product lines, or even a new business or investment opportunity without doing the homework first. It's important to remember: Making money doesn't make you smarter.

It's important to look at every opportunity with the same detached analysis as the first time you started a business. Many successful entrepreneurs have made the mistake of jumping into a new venture and blown away the equity value they generated in their original business.

It's another big mistake to avoid.

#7 Distracted by Personal Issues

Personal issues can seriously affect business performance regardless of whether they come from the owner, management or staff. Family businesses introduce particular challenges to managing personalities and corporate culture. Can you include family members in the management team without excluding others?

**In summary,
the Seven Biggest Mistakes that Entrepreneurs Make**

1. Too Entrepreneurial

2. Lack of Strategic Direction

3. Focus on Profit

4. Neglecting Key Relationships

5. Poor Marketing and Sales Management

6. "Let's do it again!"

7. Personal Distractions

But more importantly:

How do you avoid them?

The Answer

The Answer is Balance!

Each of the seven biggest mistakes is a result of the entrepreneur's failure to achieve balance between the opposing demands for his time and attention.

Avoiding these mistakes requires the entrepreneur and business owner to maintain **balance**.

- Balance Energy and Drive with Planning and Analysis
- Balance Strategic Vision with Effective Management
- Balance the Logical Head with the Intuitive Heart
- Balance Short-term Profit with Long-term Value
- Balance Personal Priorities with Strategic Objectives.

Balance these issues and avoid the *Seven Biggest Mistakes that Entrepreneurs Make* to grow and prosper in your business.

PART III
The Happy Ending

1 ▷ Find the Exit before it's an Emergency

FROM EMPLOYEE TO OWNER TO EXIT

Dave was running this meeting of the e2eForum, but we were all looking at Paul, who had just been asked by Vivian, "You're the closest to retiring from your business, Paul. What stage are you at in planning your exit strategy?"

"Thanks for reminding everyone I'm the designated Old-Timer in the group," replied Paul, with a twinkle in his eye confirming that he was still a young entrepreneur at heart. "I do have some progress to report at the end of today's meeting, though, thanks to the assistance of the much older and very wise, Uncle Ralph."

"Thanks for that introduction," I said. "I'm not sure whether to deny the 'much older' or the 'very wise' or both! How about I just share my version of the exit process for everyone here and you can share your news later. I've written the key points on the flipchart."

Preparing for exit

- **Establishing business value**
- **Enhancing business value**
- **Management succession plans**
- **Exit strategies**

"As we've already discussed, the first steps are establishing the value of your business and continuously working to improve it. Both should be done from the day you start in business, but valuation comes up most often at the exit stage. Then it's no longer a hypothetical question, it's simply, 'what price can I get for my business?'

"Unfortunately, there is no right answer to that question until somebody actually signs a cheque to buy the business. The value always depends on the particular circumstances of the buyer and the seller at the time they make the deal. Here's another brief story to give you an idea of what I mean."

IT'S WORTH HOW MUCH?

A former client with a well-established technology consulting business in Montreal called me back a few years ago to give him my assessment of the value of his business. So I did my homework. He had over twenty years of consistent profitability, a good reputation in the industry, some proprietary software products and major international corporate accounts. All that helped enhance the valuation and led me to estimate a price of $3 million to $3.5 million for his business.

He agreed that seemed reasonable, then said, "But I already sold it for $6 million."

"What?"

Then he explained that he had accepted an offer from a big European competitor in the same industry who wanted to acquire his business and had offered him $6 million. However, he discovered that once they owned it, they planned to shut it down and move the operations into their offices in Philadelphia. His employees would all be let go if they were unwilling to move. That's when he said, 'No thanks,' at any price. He did proceed with a plan to transfer shares to his key employees, based on an equity value of $4 million to ensure their loyalty and commitment to the business and give them early participation in ownership.

"As I said, the price for your business always depends on the intentions of the buyer and the seller at the time of the sale and what they want to achieve by the transaction. However, even understanding all that in advance, there are still some basic principles to establishing a price for your business."

I proceeded with my presentation on pricing and packaging your business.

PRICING YOUR BUSINESS

I usually recommend that a simple estimate of the value be included with the financial projections in every Business Plan. The principles of valuation are well known and the math is quite simple.

If you're managing the business as an owner-entrepreneur, then you should always be focused on maximizing the value of your business. That means understanding what determines the price. Not your ego-inflated value of the business, but the price that a dispassionate investor or buyer would put on it.

In establishing the value of any business, some **Basic Principles of Valuation** must be recognized:

1. The value to the owner is unique to that individual. Ego may artificially inflate the price, but the value is more often influenced by the current roles and relationships established with the owner and may change drastically with his or her departure, thereby reducing the value to a prospective new owner.

2. Value is always determined by an evaluation of the future income potential and the uncertainty or risks associated with achieving it. Regardless of the valuation method, the forecast of future income has to be credible and the potential risks have to be acceptable to get the best possible valuation.

3. Current owners tolerate more risk, uncertainty and fuzzy circumstances than new owners or investors. You may be

comfortable with the fact that you are very dependent on one critical supplier since he's an old buddy from high school; or that you have no signed lease but the landlord is your favourite uncle; or that your best sales rep is your daughter and she really wants to be president one day.

Prospective buyers will be much less enthusiastic about these issues and they should all be resolved in advance of any offer to sell.

4. Different buyers will accept different prices, terms and conditions.

   Potential buyers usually range from the passive investor looking for a reasonable return with reasonable risk; to the active investor who sees the potential to do better than you with his own management team; to the strategic investor who sees even greater opportunity in buying out a competitor, supplier or customer and merging the business with an existing company to increase revenues, eliminate redundant costs and substantially increase profits.

   The purchase offers you receive will depend on the different perceived value seen by each of these potential buyers.

In order to establish your own price for a business, several well-accepted valuation methodologies may be used. It is often a good idea to test different approaches to see what values they yield and then select a selling price that can be reasonably supported by any of the valuation methods.

P/E Multiple

The price-to-earnings multiple is a common valuation method and is widely reported for public companies listed on the stock exchange. Current price per share divided by annual earnings per share is a simple concept and is easily calculated. Unfortunately, the current

P/E multiple is not always very relevant, since the selling price today is more likely based on the expectation of future earnings and not on current earnings. The same consideration will apply to a valuation of your business.

For example, Google's share price (GOOGL) on December 31st, 2019 was U.S. $1339.39 with the previous twelve months' earnings at $45.97 per share, so the calculated P/E multiple was 29.1 times. If we used the analysts' consensus estimate for future earnings of $51.88 per share, then the adjusted P/E multiple is still a relatively high 25.8 times. Google's high multiple is based on analysts' expectations of continuing rapid growth and high profitability compared to a less exciting stock like the TD Bank.

TD Bank shares (TD) were priced at U.S. $56.13 on December 31st, 2019 with the previous twelve months' earnings at $4.81 for a calculated P/E multiple of only 11.7 times. Using the analysts' consensus estimate for future earnings of $6.88 per share, then the P/E multiple would be even lower at 8.16.

What is the P/E multiple for your company?

Typically, small owner-managed businesses can support a P/E multiple ranging from three to five. It will be higher if future earnings are very secure and not dependent on the current owner and lower if future earnings are risky and very dependent on the current owner.

The buyer will usually look at operating income, often referred to as EBITDA (Earnings before Interest, Taxes, Depreciation and Amortization), to determine profitability of the business.

If, for example, a P/E multiple of three times is applied to your $100,000 per year operating income then it will yield a price of $300,000. You might be able to get a price of $500,000, if you can persuade the buyer that a multiple of five times is reasonable and appropriate for your business.

Payback Period

Some buyers will insist on looking only at net cash flow and the payback period required to recover their initial investment and arrive at the price. They will likely have a minimum payback period, depending on risk, ranging from three to five years (which yields approximately the same price as a three to five times multiple of EBITDA, which should closely follow the annual operating net cash flow).

Discounted Cash Flow

Other investors will take the financial analyst's approach of calculating discounted Net Present Value (NPV) or the Return on Investment (ROI).

Again the future net cash flows must be forecast to arrive at a valuation. The buyer will then discount future cash flow at the required rate of return on investment, typically 15% to 20%, or calculate the expected ROI and then compare it to the required rate of return. For example, a $100,000 per year annual cash flow on a $500,000 investment provides a 20% annual return on investment.

Using these alternative methods will give you a range of valuations depending on various buyer/seller scenarios to establish your own best estimate of a fair selling price. Now you have a methodology for determining the value of your business over time. It will be useful for getting initial investors and will also help in any shareholder buy-sell agreement or succession plan.

Knowing the value of your business is a key performance measure that you should be tracking regularly. The day you need to know it should not be the first time you calculate it. Don't wait until your exit is an urgent necessity; always have a price and a plan.

As I concluded and watched the e2eForum members taking notes, I waited for the next question which usually followed.

Stan was the first to look up and ask it.

"I just did a quick calculation and I don't like the answer. So how do I improve on the price for my business?"

I replied, "You're all probably doing the first two things that enhance business value; growing revenue and reducing risk.

"The next important priority is management transition. How do you evolve from *employee to owner to exit?* It's very hard to get a new owner to buy your business if that buyer cannot replace you and your value as the owner-manager in the business. If you can transition yourself from active owner-manager to passive investor or absentee owner, it will then be much easier to transfer ownership."

PACKAGED FOR SALE

I continued, "Even if your business is not for sale, you should be planning to make it less dependent on you. Otherwise you're self-employed and not yet truly an independent entrepreneur. And *true entrepreneurs always manage their business to maximize its value –* for themselves and for future owners.

"It may not be a short-term objective to exit your business, but it is always a healthy management strategy to package your business as if it's for sale.

"That means making it independent of you, the owner, and ensuring that the performance metrics are attractive and easily understood by outsiders. Meeting those two criteria will immediately make the business more valuable and also less demanding for you to manage until you're ready to exit.

"It essentially means looking at your business as a dispassionate investor, instead of the emotionally committed owner. Step back and look at your business as it would appear to an outsider, who is trying to put a value on it. Let's review the important issues."

I returned to the flipchart and wrote a few key words for everyone to remember.

Business value is based on only two things:

1. Expected future income and
2. The degree of uncertainty or risk associated with achieving it.

The issues that affect forecast future income are:

- Market strategy, competitive positioning and branding

- Product or service plans, pricing and quality

- Cost control – both variable and fixed costs

- Asset management – cash, inventory, receivables, facilities and equipment.

Performance tracking and improvement efforts will require analysis of the financial ratios compared to your industry, specific competitors if possible, and checking trends over time. A future buyer, not to mention any banker or potential investor, will do the analysis and consider all of these factors.

The issues that affect risk in the business are:

- Reliability of financial statements
- Dependence on a few major customers or suppliers
- Dependence on key employees, especially the owner or family members
- Quality of management and employee relations
- Customer and supplier contractual relationships
- Competitive threats
- Condition of facilities and equipment

- Financial obligations, loans and leases
- Protection of intellectual property, trademarks, brand names, exclusive territories
- Potential liabilities – product failures, warranty claims, product recalls
- Regulatory issues – taxes, legal, environmental, social.

After presenting these points, I added, "You can enhance the value of your business simply by working on increasing the returns and reducing these risks.

"That usually means making the business more profitable, more stable and less dependent on you. It probably means installing a management team that can deliver the results without your direct involvement. That's always worthwhile because it will be easier for you to exit at some point in the future and reduces the demands on your time in the short term."

Packaging your business for sale immediately makes it a better business; more valuable and easier to manage.

Dave responded, "Thanks, Uncle Ralph. More good advice and a strong reminder to focus on transition to managers who can ultimately handle the whole business. Otherwise we'll never be able to cash out and exit."

"Yes," said Vivian, "and a good reminder to keep working on the strategic plan away from the preoccupation with daily details. I'm seeing more clearly that if I don't install a capable manager in my store and another vet in the clinic, I'll never develop the packaged business model that I need to move forward with my plans for franchising."

"I found that was the first step in growing my business beyond being a self-employed Web designer and programmer," said Brian.

"When I finally hired someone to do the programming, I could then focus on project management and business development. Over the last year, I've added two capable managers to handle those functions and do what I used to do. I can even take a winter break with my family in the Caribbean now. The next step is to make myself completely redundant, but I cannot yet afford to hire someone as general manager and I'm not sure whether either of the two current managers can move up to that role."

"Those challenges are all part of the process," I said. "I currently have two other clients working on their exit strategies, in addition to Paul.

"One business has a hard-working husband and wife team who have done well for themselves over many years in a small manufacturing business. Now they'd like to retire, but they've been profitable by keeping a lean team and handling all the senior management roles themselves. They have no one in place for transition to senior management. We're finding it very difficult to find a buyer for the business who is willing and able to invest in it and also manage it as well as they have. Hiring senior managers would make the business instantly unprofitable unless they can immediately increase revenues significantly.

"Another client, already in her mid-60s and looking for the exit, is in a very specialized consulting business. She has a strong well-qualified management team, but no one is interested in stepping up to the risks and responsibilities of becoming an owner, so her only option is introducing a new owner. In this case, we're looking for a merger or acquisition partner, who could integrate the current clients and consultants into an existing business with their senior management team, so the current owner can ease herself out. We're still working on the match-making.

"Those clients would all have better options if they had planned for their exit before they got to this stage."

Stan spoke up, "I'd like to have my business continue into the third generation and remain in the family, but my kids have already said no thanks. They don't want to join me in the business, so I'll have to start looking harder at management transition in my retirement plan too."

We started to pack up for the day to head back to our offices. But everyone was now preoccupied with looking into the future and thinking about two important questions:

- **How will I exit?**
- **What will my business be worth?**

They all had some new tools and tactics to work with now to answer those questions for themselves.

Wrap-up Roundtable

Before ending today's meeting, it was time for our usual e2eForum Wrap-up Roundtable with each member providing an update on their business and sharing any other news that was relevant.

WHAT'S NEW WITH YOU?

I moved the flipchart away from the conference table and looked to my left at Larry to start the wrap-up with his comments.

"Thanks to Dave," he said, acknowledging Dave sitting across the table, "for spending time to help me with my business plan. It really helped to have his feedback. Of course, I used Uncle Ralph's, *Complete Do-It-Yourself Guide to Business Plans*, but doing it yourself is still not easy." He shrugged and nodded in my direction. "Meanwhile, I'm continuing to test market the mobile application with free downloads. The feedback is helping me with both product development and finishing the business plan. I should be ready to launch in the next three to four months."

Vivian was next. "My big news is that I now have a new partner and investor in my franchise concept for the pet store and vet clinic."

There was a round of applause and, "Congrats," "Way to go Vivian!" from the other members.

"Thanks," she said. "She's an experienced businesswoman and long-time customer who has become a friend. She's really interested in helping us grow through the franchise concept. She's put in some of her own money and she brings valuable retail experience as a former senior executive in a women's fashion chain. I'm really looking forward to working with her."

Continuing around the table, we looked to Dave for his update. He said, "I'm pleased to let you know I have my increased financing finally in place, so we can expand our product lines and increase our inventories before the cycling season this year. We're also really excited about a new product line of upscale cruising bikes. They're designed for more relaxed cyclists, especially fashion conscious women who are not yet cycling, but will find these appealing, I'm sure."

"By upscale, you mean expensive?" asked Paul.

"Yes, absolutely," replied Dave with a smile. "Our target customer is upper-middle income, only mildly committed to fitness or cycling, but very attracted to fashion and design. Someone who buys the high priced workout clothes and shoes, but never goes to the gym. They already spend a lot on Lululemon or Nike high-end products, why not get them on our bikes? Early response in big city U.S. markets has been very good."

"A good example of carefully choosing a target market and going for a niche that's not yet developed," I added. "We'll look forward to learning from your experience."

"Same old, same old for me," said Paul, "but maybe I can find a niche for machined parts that will appeal to those upscale women."

"That may require a little more brainstorming," laughed Stan. "We'll look forward hearing how it works out for you."

"Maybe not a big opportunity for me," said Paul. "But for today's news, I'm happy to report that I now have a firm offer to buy my business."

"Whoa, now you have our attention!"

"It's a competitor, sort of," said Paul. "But for them it's an interesting acquisition. They don't have a shop here now. They're based in Toronto, so this would give them a new location to serve customers from and new capacity with some specialty equipment they don't have now. They've accepted the very reasonable price I was asking for and they're doing their due diligence now with a team of accountants digging deep into the numbers. I should have more news for you at the next meeting."

"It sounds like a good prospect for you, Paul. Good luck with the negotiations."

WHAT HAVE WE DONE FOR YOU LATELY?

Continuing around the table, next up was Brian.

He said, "No such thing as *same old, same old* in the Internet world. Our Web development and e-commerce software keeps changing, security is a continual challenge and the weird world of Web marketing gets crazier all the time. Everybody's posting on social media, but not many small businesses do it well and they don't have the budgets to beat the big brand names. We all just have to get better at guerrilla marketing."

"What do you mean by *guerrilla marketing*?" asked Vivian.

"It's not unique to Web marketing," said Brian, "it just means doing something unexpected or outrageous to get attention for your brand or company. To quote Uncle Ralph, '*Guerrilla marketing beats the big gorilla every time*.' Meaning that getting on the front page with a photo and a headline is always better than the full-page ad that a big brand name paid for. Richard Branson is the best at it and he says he couldn't afford to compete otherwise. Have you noticed how often he makes the news for the *Virgin Group* with a community event or outrageous stunt that gets your attention?"

"In that case I already do it!" said Vivian. "Nothing very outrageous, but we're often in the local paper for pet rescue or adopt-a-pet events and advocating for healthy pet care and nutrition – always with very photogenic cute kittens and puppies. On the other hand, we have to be careful not to venture into the political arena of the pet activists where the reaction is not always so positive."

"Guerrilla marketing is a good tactic for small business," I said. "It creates awareness with positive exposure of your business without being annoying or obnoxious. It's also important, though, to keep your guerrilla marketing consistent with your strategic positioning and corporate image. Richard Branson has established the *Virgin* brand as being innovative, fun-loving, friendly and value-oriented, and he consistently maintains that image without spending a lot on high-cost marketing campaigns. You can do the same for your business."

"Last one up today is me," said Stan. "It's been an interesting Roundtable. Sorry I don't have something more exciting for you. No air conditioners for upscale women and nobody has offered to buy my business. No good headline material at all.

"But, I do have some good news. My senior technician and project manager has said he's willing to become a part-owner. We're establishing a process for him to acquire equity over time and I think he could actually do better than me at eventually running the business. I'm starting to think about my exit strategy!"

The Member Wrap-up Roundtable was complete and proved again to be a valuable part of the e2eForum meeting.

In the confidential, non-competitive forum of peers, everyone was comfortable sharing their stories and exposing sensitive personal and business issues. It always takes a while to establish that level of confidence in each other, but it's well worth developing and maintaining.

The Wrap-up Roundtable ends our meeting together until next time. We hope you can join us again soon at another e2eForum meeting to exchange more stories between entrepreneurs.

PART IV
Enlightened Entrepreneurship

ENLIGHTENED ENTREPRENEURSHIP: THE NEED

"I'm only in it for the money."

Really? Hardly anyone admits to it; most of us are accused of it. But we know that being motivated primarily by personal gain and short-term profit are losing propositions. We must have a higher purpose and a wider range of goals and objectives to satisfy the wide spectrum of stakeholders who affect the long-term success of our businesses.

We have to consistently satisfy the needs and meet the expectations of our employees and customers, suppliers and strategic partners, governments and regulators, our communities, society and the environment. Yes, it might be called recognizing our social responsibilities and, yes, it can still be justified by the free enterprise principle of working in our own self-interest to make more money and inadvertently benefitting society at the same time.

You do not have to be a dedicated, altruistic social entrepreneur to recognize your social responsibilities. Every business has to deliver products or services with a net benefit to society and within the limits of acceptable social and environmental impacts. An enlightened entrepreneur is aware of those requirements and manages accordingly.

The need for Enlightened Entrepreneurship

My mission, whether it's providing advice to entrepreneurs or commenting on current issues, is to promote that vision of enlightened entrepreneurship. It needs to be understood, supported and encouraged by business owners and managers and the stakeholders who have a vested interest in the consequences.

I didn't invent the term, but here is my definition of **Enlightened Entrepreneurship**: *Business leadership that recognizes that doing better for the business also means doing better for employees and their families, for customers, suppliers and business partners, for communities and the planet.*

Enlightened entrepreneurs manage their businesses to achieve the economic objectives while also recognizing and meeting their social responsibilities and having a positive impact on society.

Enlightened entrepreneurs manage this way not because it is good marketing or public relations or just to feel good about themselves, but because it is the best way to build a thriving sustainable business. That expectation may seem hopelessly ambitious or naïve, but I believe it is, in fact, the only way to grow a business. We should expect nothing less.

If the entrepreneur is focused only on making money, then the consequences for everyone, including the entrepreneur, are likely to be unacceptable. Growing a business is never as simple as making short-term profits. It requires looking at the bigger picture and managing assets and people for increasing business value.

Enlightened entrepreneurship is more than a moral or ethical imperative, it is an overriding principle of good business management. It's not a new idea, it's a logical extension of the principles of building sustainable long-term value in a business by continuously satisfying all the stakeholders – employees, customers, suppliers, shareholders, governments and local communities.

Ultimately, they will decide whether they are willing to support your business success. It is never entirely up to you. So start thinking **enlightened entrepreneurship**. There is no other way that works.

ENLIGHTENED ENTREPRENEURSHIP: THE NEXT STEP

I continue to promote and recommend the concept of *enlightened entrepreneurship*, but we do not have a common understanding of the term. Some define it as a very spiritual or humanistic approach to business and others confuse it with social entrepreneurship, where the purpose of the business is to meet the social needs of society more explicitly than the economic needs of the business owners.

My concept of Enlightened Entrepreneurship:

Business leadership that recognizes that doing better for the business also means doing better for people and the planet. Enlightened entrepreneurs manage their business to achieve its economic objectives while also recognizing and meeting its social responsibilities.

Consider the meaning of "enlightened" in the historical context of the *Age of Enlightenment*, also known as the *Age of Reason*, which dominated philosophical ideas in Europe from the early 17th Century. The principal goals of Enlightenment thinkers were liberty, progress, reason, tolerance, fraternity and ending the abuses of the church and state. The ideas of the Enlightenment played a major role in inspiring both the American and the French Revolutions for freedom and democracy, giving more power to the people.

Over the last two centuries, most Western societies have experienced increasing individual freedom and less dependence on central authorities with a corresponding expansion of capitalism and free enterprise. Early in this period (1776), Adam Smith published *The Wealth of Nations* and first described the principle of the *invisible hand*, guiding entrepreneurs to unintentionally contribute to the greater good of society.

In his words, describing the business owner:

"He generally, indeed, neither intends to promote the public interest, nor knows how much he is promoting it … directing that industry in such a manner as its produce may be of the greatest

value, he intends only his own gain, and he is in this, as in many other cases, led by an invisible hand to promote an end which was no part of his intention.

By pursuing his own interest he frequently promotes that of the society more effectually than when he really intends to promote it." (Book 4, Chapter 2)

But the excesses of the industrial revolution, exploiting workers and concentrating wealth and power in the hands of only a privileged few, caused social reaction in worker revolts, the rise of trade unions and the growth of the opposing ideology of socialism.

In the 21st Century, we still observe irresponsible capitalist excesses driven by greed and selfishness that exploit workers, concentrate wealth, manipulate democracy and neglect the needs of society.

The opposing forces in society are still battling: some defending capitalism and free markets as delivering prosperity to millions of people and others blaming corporate CEOs, entrepreneurs and their political supporters for all the ills of the modern world.

We cannot keep our heads down and ignore these issues, while "taking care of business."

Enlightened entrepreneurs know that they can no longer rely on the invisible hand to help them protect the public interest and meet their social obligations and responsibilities. The modern world is more complicated and modern society is more demanding. Entrepreneurs need to be more aware and more explicit in responding to the demands of the world around them.

The next step for *Enlightened Entrepreneurship* is for us to practice it, promote it and defend it.

ENLIGHTENED ENTREPRENEURSHIP: THE ACTION PLAN

If Enlightened Entrepreneurship requires us to practice it, promote it and defend it, does accepting that mission make us missionaries?

Yes.

Your mission has a Three-Part Plan:

1. Practice enlightened entrepreneurship and lead by example.
2. Help other entrepreneurs be more enlightened and thereby more successful.
3. Advocate for enlightened entrepreneurs and help to defend entrepreneurship against the unfair critics.
   "We are not evil!"

Start with awareness followed by leadership and management that confirm the value of merging our business goals with our social responsibilities.

It is not sufficient to organize an occasional charitable event or community project to serve as a "guilt-eraser" or to counter-balance irresponsible behaviour in daily business operations. It is essential that daily business operations reflect our enlightened business culture and social values.

There will still be critics and non-believers. They cannot be ignored.

So enlightened entrepreneurs must continuously advocate, explain and defend the contributions of entrepreneurship to create a better world.

As more successful entrepreneurs join the conversation, the more convincing we will be.

We need you. So step up and join the cause.

Be a missionary for **Enlightened Entrepreneurship**.

I look forward to joining you.

PART V

Random Ramblings
from *Uncle Ralph*

Over the past decade, as your Uncle Ralph, I've written dozens of articles and Blog Posts at LearningEntrepreneurship.com and on social media through Linkedin, Facebook and Twitter. Many of the themes from those articles have been incorporated into my two business books for entrepreneurs, **The Complete Do-It-Yourself Guide to Business Plans** and **Don't Do It the Hard Way**.

For continuing updates and new ideas, information and inspiration you can visit those web sites occasionally, follow me on social media or sign up for the *Ideas for Entrepreneurs* newsletter at **LearningEntrepreneurship.com.**

For this PART V, I have selected from those past articles and revised and updated them for this 2020 Edition of **Don't Do It the Hard Way**. They present additional ideas for your consideration. Or for sharing and discussion with other entrepreneurs.

Let's start with my approach to Business Plans.

You can, of course, buy or borrow a copy of, **The Complete Do-It-Yourself Guide to Business Plans**, but as a value-added bonus with this book, here is a short summary of my approach on how to write a Business Plan that delivers the results you want.

OF COURSE YOU NEED A BUSINESS PLAN – FROM START-UP TO EXIT

Every business needs a Business Plan. It's not just for start-ups or new product launches or business expansion initiatives.

Why?

Documenting a Business Plan is an extremely useful process to focus management and owners on their business concept, their strategies and operating plans. It forces consensus and decision making that might otherwise be neglected. It requires issues to be resolved and the decisions to be reflected in the financial projections.

A well-documented business plan will help you communicate the most important elements of your strategy and plans to the people who need to know them. Including you.

Already in business for years and never needed a business plan?

It's still a good idea for all the same reasons. And now is a good time.

Ready to exit your business?
Even better. A solid business plan will be the most important document supporting the valuation of your business.

The greatest value of a business plan, however, is likely to be in the process – involving your management team in a thorough examination of your business – its purpose, its strategies and its plans to ensure success. When completed, all the key players will be more knowledgeable of the issues, the opportunities and the risks and the alternative paths considered before committing to the final plan.

Business Plan Outline and Content

Following is a suggested guideline of the layout and content for developing an effective Business Plan. It is a consolidation of best practices, based on my consulting and management experience with many different clients in a wide range of businesses at all stages from their start-up to their exit strategies.

COVER PAGE:
Includes title, date, purpose, prepared by whom, confidentiality statement, issued to whom, and a document control number.

PURPOSE:
Objectives of the Business Plan – to attract financing, key executives, customers, or strategic partners? To document strategy and action plans for all participants? Or to set the financial objectives and timetable?

CONTENTS:

1. **Executive Summary** (Maximum 2 pages; written last as a stand-alone document; it may be offered for review prior to full disclosure of the business plan and should convince the reader to go further or not.)
   - Business Concept, Plan and Objectives
   - Current status relative to the market opportunity
   - Key success factors, risks, expected results
   - Financial situation and needs
   - Reference to the complete Business Plan for more detail

2. **Concept and Business Opportunity** (Describe the need being addressed; how the approach is different and why it is likely to succeed.)
   - Market need and current solutions available
   - Business concept and product/service differentiation
   - Initial market feedback

3. **Mission statement** (Generate missionaries! Why should others join the cause – to have fun, make money, make a difference?)
   - Clear, attractive objectives – who and what do you want to be?
   - Statement of values and priorities
   - Milestones and timetable – where and when

4. **Market Analysis** (Provide relevant, pertinent information to demonstrate your knowledge and competence in the industry.)
   - The overall market, recent changes
   - Market segments
   - Target market and customers
   - Customer characteristics
   - Customer needs
   - Buying and selling process

5. **Competition** (Demonstrate an awareness of competitors and confirm your ability to compete successfully.)
   - Industry overview, recent changes
   - Nature of competition, inside and outside the industry
   - Primary competitors
   - Competitive products/services, relative pricing, advantages, disadvantages
   - Opportunities, protection by patents, copyrights, barriers to entry
   - Threats and risks, ability of competitors to respond, imitate or copy

6. **Strategic Plan** (Describe your starting point, direction, objectives and the plan to get there.)
   - Company history and background – experience, resources
   - Key competitive strengths & current weaknesses
   - Business plan and strategy to leverage your strengths and reduce the weaknesses
   - Step-by-step Action Plan for implementing the strategy

7. **Management team** (Usually the most important factor in determining your success and in attracting staff and financing. Emphasize your current strengths and your plan to fill in the gaps.)
   - Key personnel, experience & credentials
   - Staffing plan
   - Organizational structure

8. **Product & Service Offering** (Consider the reader's familiarity with the industry, avoid technical jargon; relate to the market and the competition.)
   - Product/service description

- Positioning of products/services
- Competitive evaluation of products/services
- Future products/services

9. **Marketing and sales plan** (Another key to success, too often neglected by owner/managers with strong product, technical, or operations backgrounds. Prove you have a plan that will be affordable and effective. DO NOT suggest there is no competition and the product sells itself.)
   - Marketing strategy, positioning, presentation
   - Advertising, Promotions/incentives
   - Web marketing
   - Sales tactics
   - Publicity, public relations, press releases
   - Trade shows, industry events

10. **Operations plan** (Describe the important issues and factors that will affect customer service perceptions and the required investments in operations.)
    - Production, manufacturing processes
    - Processes for product/service delivery
    - Customer service and support
    - Facilities and staff required

11. **Risk analysis** (What can go wrong, what will you do about it?)
    - Market risks – economic cycle, interest rates, currency, government regulations, trade restrictions.
    - Business risks – key customer & supplier dependence, labour availability, staff turnover, new competitors, new technology and changing demand.

12. **Financial plan** (Convert all the preceding words into numbers, for the next year by month, then three-to-five years annually.)

- Summary paragraph and with financial table and graphic
- Assumptions and disclaimers
- Starting Balance Sheet
- Profit and Loss Projections
- Cash Flow Projection
- Balance Sheet Projections
- Ratio's and Analysis, Value of equity
- Financial needs
- Sources of funds

APPENDICES:

Add some personalization and realism with biographies and photos of key executives, product photos, marketing literature, sample packaging, facility plans, press coverage, customer testimonials, relevant research documents, etc.

Following these guidelines will ensure that you have considered all the issues and can defend your strategies and action plans against all inquisitors.

A good business plan, kept current and relevant, will be a useful tool to get your business started, to manage growth and achieve your objectives and to support your business valuation for eventual sale or exit.

CONSULTANTS:
HOW TO CHOOSE, USE, AND NOT ABUSE THEM.

Since doing my first consulting project over forty years ago, I've learned a lot about how to successfully manage consulting projects and the client/consultant relationship. Here are some ideas that may help you with your consultants (and your lawyers, accountants and other professionals):

1. Before you introduce consultants to the process, be sure you **need** what you want and **want** what you need. Beware of consultants that agree to do whatever you want, whether you need it or not.

2. Look internally to confirm **the three "C's"** of consulting project readiness:

   Capacity in budget, time and resources

   Commitment of management and staff affected by the process

   Capability to support the project and implement the conclusions.

3. **One more "C" – Compatibility.** Select your consultants from an organisation with an attitude and orientation that is compatible with yours – corporate multinational or local entrepreneurial business?

4. Recognize whether your consulting needs are **strategic** — requiring outside expertise to inspire and facilitate your business planning process or **operational** — bringing practical knowledge, skills, tactics and experience that are not available internally.

5. Meet the **operating consultant**. It may not be the same charming, talented person who sold you the work. And at the fee rates they're charging you don't want to train a recent MBA, who started last week and studied your industry yesterday.

6. **Test Drive:** Check whether the consultant arrives with questions, not answers; will operate as neither boss nor employee; and will win the hearts and minds of your staff. **Successful consultants will listen, understand, empathize, analyze, strategize and persuade,** better than normal people.

7. Remember you are hiring a consultant to **challenge and push** you. You are not renting a new friend to tell you how smart you are.

8. Can you confidently expect a solution that will be **yours** not theirs?

9. Ask for **references**. Call them.

10. Ask **who** is not on the reference list and **why not**. Learn what they think causes a project to be unsuccessful. And ask which list you can expect to be on when this is over?

11. Ask for fee rates and a work plan with estimated hours. Then agree on a **fixed fee** for agreed deliverables with dates, documents and milestones.

12. Don't let their **progress reports** interfere with your progress. Get what you need, not what they need for CYA (Cover Your Ass) back at the office.

13. Check **who else** is billing time to your project. Sometimes there is a very expensive partner back at the office who needs to keep his billing rate up. Your budget can be quickly consumed while he "supervises" from a distance.

14. Avoid **surprises**. Ask about additional expenses: travel, telephone and printing. Terms of payment?

15. Do they have a satisfaction guarantee?

16. Get the agreement in writing, **read it** before signing it.

17. Watch for **signs of trouble**: such as, selling more work before the work is done; long delays between on-site visits; too much time spent "back at the office" and billed to you.

18. And finally, remember consultants are people too. They want to boast about good work and satisfied clients. You can help them help you. **Don't be difficult**.

With all due respect and best regards to all my favourite clients and consultants.

MANAGING IN DIFFICULT TIMES

Ignoring or avoiding a difficult business environment is simply not possible. It will happen, sooner or later.

A credit crisis, stock market meltdown, or a looming recession all affect the attitudes and actions of consumers, employees, investors, lenders and business managers. What are some helpful ideas to respond effectively?

Stay focused
Avoid being distracted by the bombardment of bad news.

Stay focused on customers and employees, especially the ones that you have and want to keep. Don't freeze. But don't over-react. Be calm, rational, reassuring and pro-active.

Don't just share the pain, provide relief. Misery may love company, but everybody still remains miserable if you just talk about it and do nothing. Try to be more creative and take appropriate action. Don't neglect the good news; look for the silver lining in the dark clouds – maybe currency exchange and interest rates are down temporarily, so now you can expedite foreign currency sales or re-finance some lending to improve cash flow.

Be relevant
Take a close look at your customers' changing needs and your product or service offerings. Do you have recession proof products or are they vulnerable? Costumers will be postponing or redirecting their purchase decisions in the current challenging climate. Can you keep their business with a new cost-reduced service or a more creative approach to packaging, pricing, terms and conditions?

Leverage the sense of urgency
Nobody is unaware of the current economic circumstances affecting your business. Employees are already aware of the issues and the problems in front of them, so it will be easier to get them to accept

the solutions. That means it's more likely that they are receptive to expense reductions, removing frills, postponing projects, reducing assets and conserving cash. It may be opportune to revise compensation or bonus plans, change distribution channels, move marketing programs to lower cost online approaches.

Take advantage of the sense of urgency that exists. Now is the time to resolve lingering problems; just be cautious not to do permanent damage to key employee, customer and supplier relationships that you want to retain.

Recognize the changing environment
You probably started the year under different assumptions that affected corporate budgets and business plans. Sales targets may now be unrealistic and should be adjusted downwards to maintain the rewards and motivation for top performers who continue to deliver in spite of challenging times. Try to use an external benchmark to justify the adjustment and not give the impression that you are forgiving poor performance.

Look for opportunities generated by the crisis
If you have been smart enough to stash cash and build a relatively secure business, then you can take advantage of some unique opportunities that exist. Build your team by attracting top performing employees who may be ready to move from shaky competitors into your welcoming arms. Or buy out a competitor, if the company is suddenly for sale at a bargain price. The big boys are doing it; so can you.

Talk to your banker
Make sure she is not worrying unnecessarily. Or at least worrying for the right reasons and hearing them directly from you.

If you are in better shape than most and credit is available, then increase your credit limits now to handle the potential unexpected impacts and to support the new opportunities you may want to pursue.

Avoid being the unwilling prey

Recognize that competitors may also see you in difficulty and seize the opportunity to raid key employees or buy you out at a distressed price. You need to keep close to your key employees and ensure their career plans remain with you. If you are a likely target for merger or acquisition, then start working on your choice of preferred partner and determine your business valuation under normal circumstances, not current crisis conditions. Then take the initiative before you lose control of the situation. You and your business will be better for it.

In summary:

Be brave, be flexible, be creative.

Analyze, decide, take action.

E-BUSINESS CHALLENGES FOR ENTREPRENEURS

It would unacceptable I'm sure, to write a book of advice for entrepreneurs without discussing the impact of the Internet and Web technologies on small business. So this section is meant to avoid that potential deficiency.

Since the early stages of the internet era, most small businesses have been trying to figure out how, or if, it applied to them. Like the social media issues of today. As I had some early experience with the Internet and Web applications I have been able to provide advice and direction to entrepreneurs and managers from traditional "old economy" businesses that were evaluating the potential opportunities for their businesses.

Following is a collection of some of my articles and ideas on e-business over the past two decades that were useful in providing input for those entrepreneurs and I think they are still be instructive now. I have shown the original publication dates for you to decide if they are still relevant for you. Enjoy the read and reflect on how much has changed in such a short period of time and how much has remained the same.

Although the technology changes constantly, the principles of good management do not.

THE FIRST STEP – Getting Started

© 2000

Feeling behind the times because you are not using the Internet in your business? Don't be embarrassed, you are not yet the last to sign on. In spite of all the media attention and the hard sell from Internet service and equipment providers, a recent survey indicated that although 70% of U.S. small businesses are currently connected, only 38% have Web sites. Probably even fewer in Canada.

But before you get too comfortable you should also recognize that the Internet has changed the world around you and that small businesses are the most vulnerable. They are going to be caught in the cross fire between the aggressive Internet initiatives of larger corporations that can make huge resource commitments and the brash young entrepreneurs that are boldly launching new business models to replace the old economy. You cannot afford to keep your head down and wait for it to end.

It's time to get started.

Never mind the justification – whether it's cool, your competitors are doing it, your customers want it, or your ego is pushing you – just accept the inevitability of this technology affecting your business. The risks are real and the opportunities are immense. Even though current business volumes in the Internet economy are relatively small, the growth rates are astonishing – from zero to 50 million Internet users in the first four years. There are now over 150 million users in North America plus 87 million in Western Europe and 72 million in the Asia Pacific region. By 2005, these figures are expected to be 230 million, 213 million, and 189 million, respectively. Knowledgeable and aggressive marketers like Procter & Gamble are rapidly shifting their targets to the online audience.

So carefully assess both the opportunities and the implications, and then develop an action plan to get your business online.

Start with the learning process

Get educated on the nature of the Web and the potential for your business. It simply takes an Internet connection and the time to explore. Visit the players in your own industry, but learn from other good sites as well as the ones that turn you off. Then do an assessment of your own situation.

Is your interest in business-to-consumer or business-to-business? Consider your employees, customers and suppliers. Are they connected and comfortable with the Internet? Make sure the key staff in your business are also aware of the opportunities and the requirements to succeed with e-commerce.

Keep your focus on business objectives

It is easy to be dazzled by the technology or the growth statistics. But the opportunities offered by electronic commerce should be assessed against the same business criteria you use for other investments. Any Internet initiative can be a painful and expensive exercise. Be sure it is justified by the impact on increasing sales, reducing costs, improving customer service, or enhancing competitive advantage. The goals need to be clear in order to keep up your nerve during the process.

Once the opportunities are identified, develop more specific objectives including a budget and implementation schedule. Don't try to do it all in the first step. Focus on one key area and do it well, rather than launching several tentative, incomplete efforts.

Develop a plan for your Web site to evolve through the stages from presentation, to interaction, to transactions. Decide to what extent and at what stage you will integrate the Web processes into existing operating systems.

Do not start until you have a clear understanding and a commitment to the plan from everyone affected by the Internet strategy.

Management issues go beyond the technology

Before the opportunities can be realized a number of important implications must be addressed by management. These may be described as commitment, capacity and capability. Is the project supported by all the affected management and staff? Do you have the time and financial resources? Are you capable of installing and maintaining the new technology?

Outside resources will likely be required in addition to assigning responsibility internally. Use experienced and competent experts, even though it will be more expensive than using your nephew or another enthusiastic volunteer. Their learning experience will show up in your Web site as an amateurish token effort; and it is too important for that.

There will also be new obligations to provide training and systems support, to promote your Web site, to respond to new customer demands, and to ensure Internet security. Be sure to install reporting and analysis processes to monitor and respond with the necessary changes to achieve your original objectives.

If you missed the target, adjust, reload, and fire again

Nobody gets it right the first time, so accept the fact that this is still a learning experience for everybody. Don't be intimidated by those who are just one short chapter ahead of you. If you've done your homework, you will probably avoid some mistakes that they did not.

But there will be surprises. You may find that your initial objective was to increase sales into new markets, but the biggest opportunity may turn out to be better service at lower costs for current customers. Be prepared for inquiries from places where you have no ability to deliver. Expect your current distribution channel to over-react and to worry about your selling directly from a Web site. Respond quickly and clearly because misinformation can spread very fast. Keep your own staff well informed about your plans, the results you're getting and the process to integrate Web activities into existing operations.

Once your site is up and running satisfactorily, step way back and re-evaluate the plan and the results against your new realities. Consider changing your objectives and exploiting the new economy with some completely different ways of doing business. Do some brainstorming and assess the potential for radical new approaches before launching the next step.

THE NEXT STEP – Doing it better.

© 2000

So now you have a Web site, but as Shania Twain might say, "it don't impress me much".

Don't be discouraged, it's a common feeling after the first attempt at joining the new Web-based internet economy. It is easy to spend a lot of time, effort and money to launch a new Web initiative and still accomplish very little.

But don't give up and write off the investment. Extract as much as possible from the learning experience. And give yourself credit for not ignoring the New Economy. At least you are trying to participate in the Internet gold rush that seems to be happening exactly 100 years after the original Klondike mania. Then too, a lot of brave souls suffered pain and hardship to be part of the adventure and grab their share of the wealth.

To succeed with the next step up your own Chilkoot Trail to Internet glory let's look back and learn from the experience up to this point. Were your objectives and plan clear from the start? Were you committed to the plan and to the resources required? Did you ignore the obstacles and resistance from affected employees, customers, and channel partners, instead of resolving them in advance? Could the negative feedback have been prevented? Can you now build on this experience to deliver better results?

Remember the Internet is like baseball and golf – it's not good enough to swing and hope.

You have to study, prepare, train and practice and do it a lot before you get good at it. So now that the first step is behind you let's move on to the next step – doing it better.

It's more than the wrong choice of graphics and colours

What is the source of your discontent? Aside from the time and money invested, where exactly have the results been disappointing? No visitors? Too little activity? Or just negative feedback?

Be willing to ignore the amateur critics who will happily give you their opinion on the look and feel of your site. But pay attention if there is strong consensus that says your site is badly designed, too slow, or hard to navigate. That is valuable input that can be used to make fixes and confirm that you are committed to your e-commerce strategy and that you appreciate your customers' input.

Was it the wrong destination or the wrong route?

After reviewing feedback and the site analysis reports, it's time to re-think the original objectives and the plan. Do they need revision? Should you be more ambitious, aggressive, even radical? Or should you just get the bugs out and fine tune before adding more functionality or content.

Your objectives should have a primary focus on one of the key success criteria: increasing sales, reducing costs, improving customer service, or enhancing corporate image. If progress is being made then you are on the right track. Increasing activity may be simply a matter of pumping up the marketing effort, both online and in traditional channels.

Evolve with your customers

The Internet has become a key resource in developing the customer relationship. Customer expectations have evolved. The early attraction of customers may have been based on low price and good service. That may not be sufficient to retain the customer when he or she is promised a lower price and better service somewhere else. Customer loyalty will be developed when there is also an appreciation of the additional value of your knowledge, experience and competence. But the most valuable long-term customer relationship arises when there is a strong trust arising from personal experience and recognition of shared beliefs, attitudes, and values.

This level of customer relationship can be enhanced through your Web site. It cannot be automated. No software or animated sales robot will ever replace a friendly customer service phone call or a visit from a knowledgeable, reliable sales person. But your Web site should reflect more than your products, prices, and service policies. It should reflect your corporate personality. Is it cute and perky, or calm and professional?

The technology and techniques of the Internet should be used in the same fashion you would direct your staff to deal with customers. Polite and persuasive sales people, not aggressive or annoying. Friendly and helpful customer service representatives, not young renegades lost in their own funky, high tech world.

The abuse of e-mail marketing can also make you as unpopular as the guy that sent the LOVE BUG virus around the world. Online customers have learned to appreciate the approach of permission marketing. It is as simple as explaining why you would like to have any personal information and how you will use it and then asking for permission to send a newsletter, promotions or product information via e-mail or regular mail.

Continue to monitor, adjust, and develop

A primary benefit from an online presence is the continuous and instantaneous feedback. Continue to monitor activity and performance in order to respond before bottlenecks occur. Adjust your targets and your methods to exploit the opportunities as they are presented. Launch new initiatives with a rigorous, disciplined approach to planning and project management.

You may not strike the mother lode, but you will pick up a few nuggets and avoid starving to death.

Lessons learned from an e-commerce adventure

© 2000

It is better to have tried and failed than never to have tried at all; and even more important to learn from your mistakes.

That is what I keep telling myself after having invested the time and cash equivalent to a Harvard MBA in an e-commerce start-up that has stalled and is winding down. Not a happy prospect in light of all the media pre-occupation with e-commerce success stories and the young millionaires watching their IPOs rocket into cyberspace. But the headlines ignore the more frequent stories of new e-commerce businesses that do not hit the stock market jackpot. Many of them either settle into a low-key niche or exhaust their resources and fold.

This is the story of an Internet venture that did not make the headlines, but offers some useful insights for entrepreneurs evaluating their own initiatives. The lessons learned are applicable to your own new venture or to an investment in someone else's.

In mid-1998 we launched a new company called nxtNet with the slogan, "taking you to the next level on the Internet." Very ambitious.

My partner and I both had prior successful entrepreneurial experience in computer products and wanted to start a new venture together. We decided to develop a business that would catch the next wave of e-commerce services for mid-sized companies seeking to do business on the Internet. After long discussions, searches for a unique service offering, and many draft business plans, we developed a market strategy and then chose Intershop Communications as our software development platform. This product had the advantages of being suitable for single or multiple online storefronts and offered a flexible, economical and comprehensive solution. We committed to the product and organized staffing, facilities and equipment to start training and development immediately. The two of us provided the time and cash required to get started.

By October 1998, we had an initial product with application as an online storefront for an associated computer business. At the same time, we realized that the application had wide appeal to other computer dealers and could be sold as a multi-user database service and e-commerce resource. We had developed a consolidated catalogue of 85,000 computer products from multiple distributor product databases that allowed rapid search and comparison of product information, pricing, and current sources. Users could access the catalogue from the Internet and find a product by manufacturer, category, and part number, key word or price range and immediately see the alternate sources and prices with links to more technical information, preferred dealer pricing and actual stock levels. Additional features allowed the catalogue to be customized, so that any computer reseller could present the database as his own online storefront. This option offered all the same search and product information features to retail customers and enabled online ordering at the appropriate prices.

The product offering quickly received positive feedback and strong indications of support from all the participants – resellers, distributors, and manufacturers. It was a comprehensive, powerful, and effective tool for buying and selling at all levels within the Canadian computer distribution channel. Resellers recognized the value in an online resource to save time and effort. Distributors and manufacturers saw the opportunity to promote their products, and major news publishers in the industry wanted to offer complementary online services to their subscribers and advertisers. How could we fail with all this enthusiasm and support?

While the potential for success clearly existed, everybody had the same questions and reservations – "Who is there now?" "How many are using it?" and "I don't want to pay until it's bigger."

Reasonable objections we thought, so we added features and content for free. We promoted the product with free trials and low cost subscriptions for reseller access. Then we coaxed, persuaded, sold hard and made deals. The "contra" became the standard for obtaining press coverage – free ads, mailing lists and promotion in exchange for free participation and future consideration. Activity on the Web site and catalogue grew to 3000 visitors per month with over 800 subscribers and the distributor list of computer product suppliers increased from three to twelve.

DON'T DO IT THE HARD WAY

But revenue remained near zero as most reseller subscribers declined to pay for the service. Reasons were "it should be free – let the advertisers pay", "I don't use it enough", "There are lower cost options," or "We built our own solution." The audience did not grow fast enough, even after we offered it for free, to satisfy the advertisers and content providers. Without persistent and conspicuous sales and marketing efforts, all the participants quickly lost interest. Meanwhile the costs of database maintenance, ongoing development, site hosting, Internet access, sales, marketing and administration were increasing.

Clearly the old entrepreneurial model of controlling costs and gradually growing revenue was not going to apply. We had to realign our profile to show how zero revenue and high initial costs could still lead to significant investment returns, like other well-known Internet ventures. So from early 1999 we started an aggressive search for financing, estimating our requirements at $500,000 to $1,500,000 over the next two years before achieving positive cash flow. More business plans, spreadsheets, and glossy presentations to demonstrate future valuations up to $20 million, even $40 million.

We knocked on many doors, from banks to government agencies, from angel investors to venture capital, from stock promoters to business consultants, and again received lots of encouragement, but no financing. So, as founding partners we were faced with a continuing cash drain, no relief in sight, and the limits of our own resources rapidly approaching. It was time to put the project on hold. Strategic partners or investors might still be developed to proceed with the project, but the ongoing expenditures were stopped in late 1999.

So what were the lessons learned?

We already knew that nothing ventured, nothing gained. We now also knew that big successes in the new economy require big investments. Entrepreneurs may start small, but large investments will be required from new sources to achieve significant success. And no one will put significant money into a venture unless it is the only remaining requirement. The concept, product, development, marketing and staffing all have to be in place before an investor will provide the final ingredient – his cash. Exceptions are likely only where the management team has already succeeded in the same arena, or the new investor can also deliver the missing elements such as customers or management skills. No investor is going to take the chance that the entrepreneur with a good concept or product will also be able to deliver the required management and marketing skills to succeed after he has the cash.

Next time we will know better. And there are side benefits from this expensive learning experience. I can now admit that with the knowledge gained through our association with Intershop Communications, I was confident enough to make an investment in their stock on the German Neue Markt stock exchange at 65 Euros last year. It went over 400 Euros last month and is still rising with their rapid growth and the prospect of a NASDAQ listing this year. Almost enough to recover my investment in nxtNet. *(Authors note: I was lucky enough to cash out before the stock fell back to near zero a few years later. Intershop was not a long term success story either.)*

So the most important lesson is that education in the new economy is essential and not free, but it can lead to success outside the original plan.

Learn, be aware and be aggressively opportunistic.

Lessons Learned from Both Sides of the Digital Divide
© 2007

I have learned some important lessons from my experience on both sides of the digital divide – as a peddler of technology services and as a client of technology providers.

In the new world of the Web and E-commerce opportunities these lessons are important to keep in mind:

1. The first wave of Internet investment was driven by fear and greed.

2. Current e-business plans require more than a bright idea and a high "burn rate."

3. Success requires a strategy and a plan before jumping into action.

4. People and supporting processes are <u>always</u> more important than the technology.

5. Cool technology is a distraction; focus on the business objectives – sales increases, cost reductions, service improvements, and enhanced corporate image.

6. **The secret of success is to turn the WWW upside down – think MMM: Manage, Market, Monitor.**

7. Stop worrying about what your Web site <u>looks like</u>, start worrying about what it <u>does</u>.

8. Focus less on what it costs and more on how it pays.

9. You cannot automate <u>outstanding</u> customer service – it requires the personal touch of real people.

10. No matter how good the product is, it <u>never</u> sells itself.

11. E-mail marketing works if it's welcome to the reader; don't be a SPAMMER.

12. Viral marketing works even better: "Try it, tell a friend, win a prize."

13. Guerrilla marketing works better than gorilla marketing. (Getting attention on the front page will beat a full-page ad every time.)

14. When cash is short and you can't find OPM (Other People's Money) try contra deals. (Exchange your products and services for other consideration without exchanging cash.)

15. It's easier to get outside financing if you don't need anything else.

16. Beware of unwilling and unwelcome partners. Look for intelligent and sympathetic capital.

17. Be patient in the search for investors. Expect many "No's" before getting to a "Yes."

18. Remember the risks are real, but the opportunities are huge. (i.e. We're still driven by fear and greed.)

E-business Opportunities with Web 2.0

© 2009

Our mission as business consultants at DirectTech Solutions is to advise, inform and inspire business owners and managers and we offer these ideas for your consideration.

Have you been neglecting the e-business opportunities for your business?

In the early days of the Internet and e-business solutions the message was to "Catch the wave or be drowned by it". Every business was being told to get on the Internet to survive or stand back while the "new economy" took over their industry. Hype and hysteria were used to persuade entrepreneurs and investors to put large amounts of money into their e-business initiatives. They were motivated by either fear or greed.

Then the "old economy" rules hit the dot.com ventures and the bubble burst. Many investments ended badly. Some could be written off as an expensive learning experience. Some were just bad investments.

The hype and hysteria died and many businesses decided they could go back to business as usual. *They were wrong*.

The Internet revolution continues, albeit more quietly. The hype now focuses on *Web 2.0* with highly interactive web sites and user generated content. Huge values are being placed on high traffic sites as they are acquired by Google, Microsoft, or the media moguls, but you don't have to be a media or Web-based business to take advantage of Web 2.0.

The businesses that are leveraging the Internet most effectively are those that use Web marketing to attract business and use online services to build strong loyal customer relationships.

Those are the e-business opportunities not to be neglected. Here are some ideas to consider for using the new Internet in your business:

1. Try a search to see what a potential new customer will find if she Googles your name, your company or your product brand names. You may discover, like I did when shopping for a new BBQ that the most popular site is one full of customer complaints about "a dangerous piece of trash nobody should ever buy!" How would you like that to be the first impression for a new prospect? Or maybe you'll find a comment like the time I checked a hotel on tripadvisor.com and read "put a fork in your eye before booking this hotel!" So be sure you know what potential buyers are finding through search engines. It may give you an incentive to improve the search ranking of the sites that you would prefer they find.

2. Remember that *search engine marketing* is more than putting keywords on your site and hoping to be found by new customers. Optimizing your web site for search engine effectiveness is a complex process and it is worthwhile to consult an expert. If the most common search terms are dominated by bigger competitors, the most effective strategy may be to target a very specific market niche that is not already over-served by competing Web sites. Or use geo-targeting to focus on your local market.

3. Also consider *sponsoring carefully selected keywords* that will deliver interested prospects. People searching for those keywords are motivated potential buyers. Again there are many issues to assess, but you can start with a small budget and learn from the results to continuously improve the performance.

4. You may also want to *monitor and participate* in some of those sites that talk about products like yours and add your own two cents worth. Just be careful to maintain integrity speaking for yourself or your company. Do not make the mistake of pretending to be a delighted customer. Others have already experienced that PR disaster.

5. Many of the new Web 2.0 oriented sites attract very focused groups of site visitors who actively participate in the site. Some of them may align very well with your target market and be very productive for your placement of *relevant online advertising*. For example, if your target market is young Canadian women, then look at Divine.ca.

6. ***What about a Blog?*** A personal diary on the Web is probably not helpful to your business unless you are already a celebrity. But you may want to make yourself ***more visible and available*** and to establish yourself as an ***expert resource***. Both objectives can contribute to building stronger customer relationships. A Blog site will also improve your search engine rankings if it reinforces the same keywords and is linked to your company site and others that are relevant. It does impose the obligation, though, to keep adding new content. See my website Blogs and links to others for some ideas. Or try it yourself at Blogger.com.

7. Maybe you should create a ***Blog for your customers?*** Setting up an online users group might be helpful to exchange ideas and input while creating a higher level of brand loyalty and commitment.

8. Also consider Web 2.0 applications to ***reduce your costs and improve your services.*** The available applications have evolved to deliver more for less. Powerful and easy-to-use sales force automation and email marketing services are available from providers like Salesforce.com and Constant Contact.

9. Your ***customers and employees*** may be very comfortable with all the latest applications - Blogs, social networks, user generated content, RSS feeds, Podcasting, Twitter, and Wikis. Their ***expectations are high***. Can you productively integrate any of these applications into your e-business strategy? If you do not, is there a risk that a competitor or a new approach will lead customers away from you?

Much has changed on the Internet, but neglecting it is not an option.

You will have noticed that the sermon on e-business from me or anyone else has not changed much in twenty years. Essentially, be aware of the possibilities; keep up with customer expectations; have a plan that is appropriate to your budget, capabilities and business model; then do it. Those principles apply whether you are finally upgrading your first website are you are now trying to enhance your online performance with a social media campaign.

In summary, although Internet technologies and applications have evolved incredibly in the twenty years since we first connected and in the decade since Facebook started, the sound management principles for applying the Web to your business still apply.

The Internet names and numbers may have changed, but the advice has not:

- Your online initiatives must be an integral part of your business plan.

- Thorough preparation and good project management are essential to achieving a satisfactory return for investments online.

- Continuously monitoring the real-time feedback and analytics will allow you to review, respond and revise your plans for improved results.

Start with a diagnostic of your current online performance, check the competitive environment and then come up with a plan to do better.

HENRY MINTZBERG IS WORTH LISTENING TO

I had the pleasure a few years ago of hearing a presentation by Henry Mintzberg, McGill professor and management guru.

One attendee described him as the "Tiger Woods of management science." I know him as the Strategy Professor from my McGill MBA of 40-plus years ago. *(Yikes! Neither of us seem to have aged that much. OK, greyer for me and less hair for him.)*

Henry is a widely respected academic and the acclaimed author of The Nature of Managerial Work, The Rise and Fall of Strategic Planning, Managers not MBAs and many other books and articles that argue against the conventional wisdom and provoke thoughtful reflection on management and business. He is also the co-founder of the International Master's Program in Practicing Management (IMPM), a unique approach to learning that is designed to flow from the shared experience of participants.

His presentation was originally advertised to be on the dilemma of corporate compensation, but that turned out be only part of his critique of the modern CEO. His criticism was directed more at the continuing focus on shareholder value that was a factor in the great recession of 2008.

Some of his points worth considering:

- Productivity is a euphemism for cutting costs, mostly by firing employees (he calls it "modern blood-letting"), while maintaining short-term revenues.
- The theoretical corporate objective of maximizing long-term shareholder value has been hijacked to mean pushing short-term earnings to inflate current market share prices.
- How can employees be motivated to work for shareholders they have never met? Many of whom have no interest in the

company except for the short-term ability to make a profit on their investment – they are mostly day traders or hedge funds.

- Shareholder value is not a worthy objective of the corporate institution as it specifically ignores (or exploits) other stakeholders, especially employees.

- Mercenary corporate leadership is stealing from shareholders with absurd compensation and severance packages that are not tied to performance. "The robber barons are back!"

- The old corporate silos have been replaced by horizontal slabs of concrete separating executives from their employees and the real operating issues.

- "Human resources" is a term that dehumanizes human beings. It makes it easier to treat people like other "resources," to buy, sell, use and dispose of. It's like describing airline passengers as "self-loading cargo!" (Quoting a client he had worked with.)

- Corporations need to remember that customers are people too. They are not just another asset to be exploited.

Professor Mintzberg also suggested some remedies to avoid another recession like we had in 2008:

- Stop being misled by the apparent productivity gains and profitability of large American corporations.

- Get the mercenaries out of the executive suite and add employee voices in the boardroom.

- Stop running businesses to satisfy financial analysts or investors with no interest in anything except short-term results.

- Install real corporate leadership that is concerned, engaged, and modest. *(Interestingly close to Jim Collins' description of Level Five Leadership in Good to Great.)*

- Ignore the obsession with measurable factors and reconsider the immeasurable - values, benefits and impacts of economic activity.

- In the larger context, get back to a better balance of the three sectors in society – public, private and social.

His full commentary and other thought-provoking ideas and analysis are available at *Mintzberg.org*

Lots to think about and issues to influence if we can.

THE BEST ADVICE I EVER GOT

In three words: DON'T WASTE TIME.

In providing the following background story, I may appear to be ignoring that advice by taking more time to write about it and requiring you to take more time to read about it.

But the advice is really about making choices on how to use the limited time available in one lifetime. It does not exclude learning, relaxing, or quiet contemplation instead of continuous frantic activity. In this case, I am choosing to reinforce the message and help make it memorable by telling the story (in keeping with the theme of this book) and you may choose to read it for the same reasons.

I was at UBC in Vancouver in 1964, my first year in Engineering. All first-year engineers were given the Engineering Handbook providing all the advice and information we needed to successfully complete the following four years of study. The book was full of useful material and started with welcoming comments from the Dean of Engineering, the University President and other dignitaries with all the usual flowery clichés expected in these messages.

One page was reserved for Steve Whitelaw, President of the Engineering Undergraduate Society. Steve was a popular President with a reputation as a very bright, creative leader. That reputation was based on his leadership in a number of engineering student stunts that made the national news, like the time they kidnapped another university's mascot or hung a VW beetle from the Lion's Gate Bridge.

His biggest coup was bringing to a conclusion the long campus debate over some weird concrete modern-art sculptures that appeared one-year on compass. They had received the scorn and contempt of 'ignorant and uncultured' engineering students, but were vigorously defended by the arts faculty and administration.

The intensity of the debate exploded on campus and in the local newspapers on the day the engineers went on a rampage and completely destroyed all the sculptures leaving them in heaps of broken concrete and steel. That's when Steve finally advised everyone that the engineers had built and installed them all in the first place.

So his advice in the Engineering Handbook would have received our attention.

It was a blank page with his signature and the three words:

DON'T WASTE TIME

Call it leading by example.

WHAT CAN ENTREPRENEURS LEARN FROM THE OLYMPICS?

Aside from enjoying the great spectacle of the Summer or Winter Olympic Games and the thrill of witnessing historic athletic accomplishments, there are also some important concepts and ideas that we can learn from Olympic athletes and apply to our businesses.

Consider these approaches to managing your business better:

The four year planning horizon
Set aside your current plan. Review your results from last year and define new "Olympic record" performance objectives for the next four-year cycle with a plan and specific milestones for each year.

Focus on your strengths
Choose to compete in the areas where you are most likely to succeed. Most Olympic athletes specialize. Even multiple medal winners don't try more than a few events within their specialty. Accept that you can't be great at everything, just few important things that happen to match your greatest strengths.

Make good decisions
You have to make choices to either give it your best effort over a long period of time, or quit. Make good choices. Know when and what to quit.

Push your limits
Test your capabilities and endurance to the maximum. "Tear and repair" is the way to build strength and endurance in muscle tissue; maybe in your organization too.

Learn from the leaders
What do the top competitors do that you can also do? Look at their preparation and training techniques; the little things that add up to a big difference on race day.

Learn from your losses

Study your own performance and learn what makes the difference between your best results and your second best.

It's not for the money

You have to love it passionately enough to do what it takes to be a winner. The money will follow if you have the passion and persistence to excel.

There is only one gold medal

You may have to settle for being the fourth or the sixteenth best in the world at what you do. That is still impressive and makes you better than a lot of your competitors.

Prepare for upsets

The best competitors know how to deliver for the big events and usually avoid surprises. They also know not to underestimate their competition. Maybe you can be the upset winner when the opportunity arises, if you are well prepared and committed to maximum performance when it's required.

Have a world class support team

Coaching makes a difference. Check that your consultants, advisors and support staff are up to Olympic standards.

Don't cheat

The short-term glory of victory will eventually be replaced by the long-term disgrace of breaking the rules.

It's never too late

Canadian equestrian Ian Millar won a medal at age 61 after competing in nine Olympics. American swimmer Dara Torres at age 41 won three silver medals at the Olympics after coming back from retirement. Veterans can still compete and win. Don't be intimidated by new competitors. Stay in the game and play to win.

Now go enjoy the next Olympic Games and learn a few more lessons of your own.

SALES MANAGEMENT STRATEGY SIMPLIFIED

- **Sales objective** is to move prospects to buyers.

- **Sales process** is to take leads identified by marketing, qualify them as prospects, make the sales presentation and get the order.

- **Sales Rep** needs to be known, liked, trusted and respected for sales success.

- **Sell** the rep, then the company, then the product.

Keep it simple

COLD CALLING – LEARN TO LOVE IT!

Most of my advice for entrepreneurs is strategic, practical and relevant, but does not cover detailed operating instructions on how to proceed. This article is different.

At several stages of my career, particularly as an independent consultant, I have been responsible for my own business development and had to master the dreaded process of cold calling. I developed my own methodology, discovered I was good at it and had surprisingly good results.

I learned to love it and was asked to share my ideas with a local business networking group of self-employed solo entrepreneurs. Most of them hated cold calling and knew they were not good at it. These are the takeaway notes that I provided for the presentation.

PURPOSE OF COLD CALLING

1. Develop new business with targeted prospects.
2. Make yourself known to people you don't know and who don't know you.
3. Networking is not enough.

THE PROCESS

1. Have a strategy and a plan with a clear offering and a well-defined targeted market.
2. The best results start with a good quality prospect list.
3. Sales process: Generate Leads, Qualify Prospects, Close Opportunities, deliver the Service, Build Relationships and Grow your Business.
4. Move new contacts from awareness, to knowledge, to understanding of your business.

5. People prefer to buy from people they like, respect, and trust. Build a relationship by meeting those needs in that sequence.

6. During the call, sell yourself first, then the company, then the product.

7. While your purpose is to sell, don't neglect to identify valuable friends and influencers who may lead you to more prospects.

8. Big numbers still yield small results, bigger numbers yield better results. **Make the calls.**

9. If you cannot or will not do cold calls, then hire someone who is good at it and likes to do it. Let them set appointments with qualified and interested prospects that are willing to meet you.

10. Make cold calling an important part of your integrated marketing communications plan – networking, PR, advertising, direct mail, e-mail, and Web marketing.

TECHNIQUE

1. Be prepared before you start. Organize your desk and your thoughts.

2. "Look sharp, feel sharp, be sharp".

3. Think enthusiastic and you'll be enthusiastic.

4. If you're bored, you're also *boring*. **Don't be boring!**

5. You can hear a smile over the telephone.

6. If they like you, maybe they'll listen.

7. Keep it simple. "You wanna buy a book?"

8. This is a sales call, not a social call.

9. Remember where you are in the process, don't sell too soon.

10. You are qualifying them, while they are qualifying you.

11. Be patient, polite, and persistent.

12. Listen before you speak. It's a conversation, not a speech.

13. Take advantage of voice mail.

14. Let the assistant assist.

15. Have a script. **Do not read it.**

16. Close with an agreed action step.

17. Keep score and keep updating your contact lists.

SCRIPT

Be prepared:

1. Have a good quality contact list.

2. Have your sales materials and agenda ready to respond.

3. Practice your response to the expected objections.

4. Check the prospect's website for info on the company and identify more specific potential requirements for your products or services. You will then sound more like you have carefully selected them before calling. (Be careful not to critique before you compliment.)

SAMPLE SCRIPT OUTLINE

Hello, my name is _____ I'm the *(President/Sales Mgr. ...)* of _____. *(I'm calling because...)*

We are *(introducing, offering...)* and I wanted to present to your company *(our best solution for you ....)*.

(Ask the leading question that will generate "yes" to qualify the prospect) Do you have this problem or ever use ...?

(Be prepared to explain/persuade why he/she has a need and you have the answer.)

We have recently ... for companies like yours...

Our clients love us because ...

(Remember you are still <u>qualifying</u> this contact, so ask the right questions. ... Is this the right person to decide, do they ever use your type of product/service, do they have the budget, is now the right time to make a purchase?)

(Try to identify who, what, when are the best prospects on your list. If there no prospect of a sale or a very low probability – "Thank you & goodbye." Remove them from your lists and avoid wasting more time.)

(If it's a good prospect, and a good probability of doing business soon, move on to the follow-up action item.)

Can we meet next Tuesday at 3:00PM to discuss how we might help to achieve ...? I'll bring/prepare.... specifically for your need..., just *as we just discussed.*

(If it's not a likely prospect now, then keep the contact open for future opportunities, or referrals, by requesting permission to follow up by mail, e-mail, or telephone.)

Close:

(Summarize and confirm the follow-up that you plan.)

1. OK, thank you for your time, we'll take your name off our contact list.

2. OK, thank you for your time, I'll follow up **as agreed.**

3. Great, I'll see you on Tuesday at 3:00PM

And on to the next one.

Happy selling!

HOW ARE WE DOING SO FAR?

At any time during the year, you may find yourself looking back and thinking, *OK, we could be even worse off, but let's hope it gets better from here.* For most of us, the negative impacts of external conditions on our business are unpredictable, inconsistent and inconclusive.

So what are the right management strategies and action plans to get through the economic turmoil and uncertainty with a more resilient and stable business?

Here are the lessons we've learned from our clients, commentators and experts, applicable anytime in any year:

1. Do not rely on the headlines.

The media are just trying to get your attention and a train wreck is always more attention-grabbing than a success story. They will provide neither balanced reporting nor insightful analysis for input to your planning or decision making. You will have to dig deeper. Make sure your market data and competitor intelligence is current and accurate.

2. Communicate. Communicate. Communicate.

Keep employees and customers informed. They may be worried, confused and need to be reassured that they can count on you. You may not have good news for them, but they will appreciate hearing directly from you and are not being left guessing what's coming next.

3. Keep on Selling.

Now is not the time to cut back on marketing and sales. Your efforts now will be more even conspicuous and effective if your competitors back out of the market and away from their customers. Be selective and very focused. Work on building stronger customer relationships by being relevant and responsive to the current economic circumstances. Avoid the "cry for help" advertising that only confirms "we're desperate and need the sales." Customers are looking for strength, not weakness. Calmness, confidence and competence are much more appealing to potential buyers who are still growing and want reliable, long term suppliers.

4. Do quickly what obviously needs to be done.
If it's clear to you it's also clear to the people affected. They are waiting for you to act and will be more confident and proactive themselves, if they see you taking action. Face the facts, don't fight the facts.

5. Adapt.
Remember Darwin's "survival of the fittest": those who adapt to their environment are most likely to survive; not the strongest or the biggest. This is not the time to be stubbornly persistent about your plans. Look around and be creative. Your destination may still be the same, but the route, the vehicle and the passengers may need to be changed.

6. Be confident, but cautious.
Recognize the difference between calculated risk and a state of uncertainty. Make a decision if the potential outcomes and their probabilities are reasonably clear, but hold fire if they are not.

7. Show conspicuous leadership.
President Barack Obama understood the concept of being the most conspicuous spokesman for his plans and policies. No one can do it better than the one who is ultimately responsible. We may not all be as adept at communicating as he was, but we can all speak with more sincerity and integrity on our concerns, our strategies and our plans than any spokesperson or intermediary.

Good management will be tested during these difficult times, but good decisions now will mean a better business for the future. Keep at it. The hard times too will pass.

A 10 POINT DIAGNOSTIC FOR YOUR BUSINESS

From my experience, most businesses can benefit from a regular health check – a business diagnostic that takes a thorough look at the whole business and identifies priorities and potential solutions for better performance.

Maybe you already have an annual budgeting or strategic planning process, but a regular business diagnostic can be a very valuable additional exercise. Step back from the daily demands on your time and look at your business from a distance to re-assess how well you're doing in the key areas that affect success.

Here is a list of **10 check points** and some approaches to consider for raising your business performance to the next level:

1. Start with a strategic plan. You and your team need to be chasing the same dream. Write it down or find your last business plan. Review it against last year's results. Re-write it. Use it. It's the road map to achieving your business objectives. But remember that reaching your goals is more important than the route you take.

2. Ensure that all your managers **use your documented business plan** as their guide to corporate strategy and management. Develop personal goals and individual project plans against corporate objectives. Monitor results throughout the year. Include your own performance against your objectives.

3. You're in a competitive business: **Are you keeping score?** Compare your key performance indicators to industry averages and the top performers and develop a specific action plan to achieve better results.

4. Evaluate your performance in customer service and building long-term loyal relationships. Before you accept the assessment of your own staff, ask your customers for their opinion. Identify the key areas for improvement. Improve them.

5. What about the people you need most and who know you best: **your employees?** Try a blind survey to get feedback on what they really think about the company, culture, compensation, communications and your competition. Do they still believe you're a **great place to work?**

6. Assess your degree of satisfaction with each of the **six P's in your marketing mix** - Product, Positioning, Promotion, Price, Packaging, and Placement. Fix what's broken.

7. Assess your **corporate image** against the biggest and best brands in your business. Look at all your literature and your Website. Do they make you look as good as you really are? Are they off the mark? Raise your image to a higher levels of awareness. Live up to it.

8. Re-evaluate your website. Are your competitors raising customer expectations? To improve your own results **turn the WWW upside down** and think **MMM** – Manage, Market, and Monitor. Do it better. Don't wait to be asked.

9. Re-read all your marketing communications. Do they capture the **four C's – current, clear, concise and consistent**? Eliminate the misinformation and throw out what doesn't work anymore. Ensure **your marketing message** is consistent with the pitch of your most successful sales reps.

10. Review the use of **information technologies** in your business. Are they part of the solution or part of the problem in productivity and performance? Complete a strategic review of your technology needs using a qualified, objective outside resource before buying the next solution that appears to solve all your problems. It takes an expert.

Share these ideas with your business associates and use them to improve your performance. There should be fewer areas to improve on next year when you do the business diagnostic.

BE PRUDENT NOT PARANOID

Soon after starting my business in computer products distribution, I got burned by a couple of retailers passing bad checks. Whether they were dishonest or just bad managers, the result was the same: Whack, NSF!

I was an inexperienced young entrepreneur, so it was easy to over-react and go beyond caution to become suspicious and distrustful of every customer. Not a good idea. I started to notice that the sales reps and customer service staff were following my lead too well. Aggressively pushing for cash-on-delivery or making unreasonable demands before accepting any sales on credit.

Now we had a new problem. Customers were getting turned off and going elsewhere to competitors who were easier to do business with.

We adjusted our attitudes and went back to dealing in good faith and treating customers and other business partners with more respect. That means trusting them implicitly and expecting the best of intentions. If problems arise, it's better to ask than to assume the worst. Maybe you can work it out.

It's not counting on blind faith or being naïve. Prudent practices are still necessary and that includes clear and agreed terms and conditions before you do business.

Be aware of the risks of doing business and then manage them. Unfortunately, they cannot be avoided. Unless you lock the doors and don't answer the phone.

IT'S ANOTHER NEW YEAR. SO WHAT.

You have already looked at too many year-end reviews and predictions for next year. The consensus seems to be that last year was bad everywhere and next year will be worse: more terrorist events and political stupidity, extreme weather and natural disasters, wildly fluctuating market values on all your investments and challenging economic conditions for every industry.

So, if you cannot control the world around you what can you do differently this year?

A good general rule is to keep it simple. Focus on just two memorable accomplishments for the year – one personal, one professional. Richard Branson suggests that you refrain from making another *To-do* list, but work instead on your *To-be* list. It is more important who you are than what you do.

Work on making memories.

If you look back on last year, how would you characterize it? Personally and professionally what were the outstanding memories? Did they just happen or were they your intent? For me personally, it was the year of settling into a new condo and adjusting family relationships. Professionally, after a long and complicated four-year process, we finally concluded on the sale of a client's business. Nothing that changed the world, but significant events for people important to me.

So what will be your memories and your influence on the memories of the people important to you for the coming year? My intent is to make a first trip to Africa in an ambitious year of travel adventures and to advance the cause of enlightened entrepreneurship with more advocacy through my writing projects and speaking events.

I wish you well with your own plans for a better you and for good memories of the coming year.

Of course, good wishes are not sufficient. More detail is required in the to-do lists and work plans, schedules and budgets, but I prefer to start with some simple objectives that are easy to remember without getting distracted by "other events." I recommend the same approach to you.

Have a good year. Make it memorable.

FORGET FORECASTS – THEY'RE USELESS.

Each year there comes a time when everyone seems compelled to make forecasts. Experts and amateurs all have opinions and predictions they want to share. The experts try to decide whether to play safe and predict more of the same or to get more attention and predict something radical — Canadian dollar will go down to 59 cents U.S! Oil prices will rise back up to $100!

We should ignore them all. Their forecasts are useless.

I have worked on many forecasts myself, in plans and projections for my own businesses and for clients. They're always creative fiction. Supported by research, rigorous analysis and impeccable logic, but still unlikely to accurately predict the future.

It's useful to remember before starting that all forecasts are meant to convince ourselves or someone else what we expect will happen. It would be better to describe them as "reasonable expectations" or to use the engineering term – SWAG estimate – Scientific Wild-Ass Guess.

All we know for sure is that the forecasts will be wrong. We just don't know by how much or in which direction.

So if we cannot predict the future, what can we do?

Our primary objective should be to understand our business environment – the competitive landscape and the economic conditions. The real issues to research and analyze are the trends, the causes and effects, the alternative scenarios we need to be prepared for and the most likely ones to occur. Then we have something we can work with.

Happy forecasting!

SOLD! YOU THOUGHT IT WOULD BE EASY?

Three challenging steps to selling your business

If you're thinking of selling your business someday, remember it's a long, complicated process that you should start well in advance.

The recent sale of a client's manufacturing business, reminded me once again that a successful sale requires considerable time and effort – before, during and after the deal is made. Rigorous planning and preparing for the sale, working hard to get the price and terms you want, then closing the deal and managing the transition to new ownership.

This deal began about five years ago with the casual comment, "I'm thinking it's time to sell. What do you think my business is worth?"

Always a challenging question, loaded with high expectations and a lot of ego. I did the analysis and presented my estimated range of potential values based on standard valuation techniques. As usual, the owner was disappointed with the number, but was eventually persuaded that the rationale was reasonable.

It helps to ask, "How much would you pay to buy this business if you were not already the owner?"

It helps to remember an important basic principle behind any financial transaction.

Every investment requires an assessment of value based on the expected rate of return and any sale only happens when the buyer values it more than the seller. Never when it's the opposite.

A mutually agreed price will be somewhere below the buyer's highest valuation and above the seller's minimum price.

Pride and ego can persuade the owner to price the business much higher than any rationale buyer can justify or be willing to pay. We could look for a foolish person with lots of money, but the two are not often found together.

So, once the decision to sell is made, what are the three steps required to sell your business?

First Step: Packaging for Sale

If you have decided that the current value of your business is not sufficient to accept an offer to sell it at that price, then you have to work on an action plan to increase the value and make the business more presentable to prospective buyers.

The value is always increased if the business can improve on net income and reduce the risk associated with sustaining it. The immediate requirements to stabilize revenue, reduce costs and clean-up the balance sheet are usually obvious, if looked at from the perspective of an outside investor. But often the most difficult and important issue to be resolved in order to enhance the value of the business is to reduce its dependency on current ownership. That may mean introducing a stronger management team and removing the owners from an active role. You cannot sell and exit the business, if it will fail immediately after you leave. (Seems obvious, I know.)

Ideally, the business should already be managed to make it as valuable as possible by continually addressing the key issues of sustaining growth, reducing risk and building a strong management team. When those issues are all reasonably resolved and the tough questions can be answered, then you are ready to start presenting your business for sale.

Second Step: Presenting for Sale

Preparing for sale requires some strategic planning. We need to know how to present the business for sale and to which potential buyers.

Strategic buyers will always pay the best price because they will achieve synergies in reduced overhead or expanded sales that will add to their return on the investment and consequently to their perceived value. Who are they and where do we find them? Would you consider selling to a competitor? What if they plan to buy your business to shut it down? Are you willing to consider passive investors who are seeking high returns and low risk and will probably offer the lowest price? Would a new owner-management team be a better scenario for continuity of the business and a smooth management transition?

What are your preferred terms to maximize the after-tax cash value to you and to accelerate the payout? What is negotiable and what is not? When these strategic questions are answered you can prepare a marketing pitch and Offer for Sale to attract interested and qualified buyers.

The package should have enough information to appeal to an investor without disclosing too much confidential or competitive information. You may even wish to remain anonymous and have the initial package presented by an agent or business broker. After the prospective interested buyer has been qualified and signed a non-disclosure agreement, then a more detailed package should be available to provide the company background and financial history and support the valuation and asking price.

As proposals are exchanged and alternatives are considered, negotiations can begin. There may be many discussions and negotiations with prospects that do not lead to an accepted offer, but eventually a deal gets made. Unfortunately, you're still not done.

Third Step: Closing the Sale
The third step, closing the sale, requires completing the transaction and making the business transition to new management.

This final step can be a grinding process with all the conflicting, complicated and costly input of your accountants, lawyers and bankers. (Of course, they should all have had some prior warning and the chance for input before the deal is signed, but now it gets more serious.)

You will need professional expertise to properly document and process the negotiated Buy/Sell Agreement to avoid any subsequent liabilities, minimize the tax consequences and maximize the cash payout. You will get conflicting advice, especially from the buyers' advisors, as the best terms and conditions for you may not be in their best interest. More negotiating and compromises will be required.

Then, once the deal is properly documented and the closing gets done as planned, the parties can all work together on the transition to new management and ensure that the business stays on track for continued profitable growth and any balance of sale gets fully paid. Then you can make your graceful exit and focus on managing, or spending, all that cash.

Do you expect to sell your business *someday*?

Then it's time to get started on the first step.

PIPELINES AND POLITICS
Irrational decision making

I never studied Political Science, but as an engineer and graduate in Applied Science, I am inclined to think that there is little science involved in political decision making. Lots of ideological fervour and applied psychology, but very little scientific analysis and rational decision making.

Mom had it right when she told me, after listening to my speech to voters during my campaign for Member of Parliament in the home town riding, "Don't confuse them with the facts, they've already made up their minds."

The issue regularly attracting the most irrational political decision-making appears to be any plan to build oil and gas pipelines. Mixing vehement political rhetoric into the analysis and review process may make it more interesting and entertaining, but unfortunately does not enable decisions based on the facts and does not allow for compromise to arrive at practical solutions. Opponents with competing ideologies and political agendas use the process to beat each other up instead. Oil and energy pipeline projects are under attach all over North America. The activists just choose their preferred battering ram and keep on pounding.

Everyone starts attacking the character of their opponents and accuses them of sinister conflicts of interest. Nobody seems to be interested in listening and learning in order to find common ground and reasonable alternatives that could satisfy all parties. At least not while the media are paying attention.

> "They're just greedy oil executives who want to rip us off and destroy the planet for their immoral profits and obscene pay packages!"

"They're just eco-activist hypocrites with a vested interest in attacking capitalists and trying to kill the oil industry at any cost!"

The politicians are forced to choose sides and decide on the path that will be most popular with voters in the next election. Much like the business executive who makes bad decisions based on short-term results or the preferences of dissident shareholders, rather than managing for long-term sustainability of the business.

In both arenas, there is a disappointing lack of real leadership and decision-making based on rational analysis and the likely long-term consequences for people and the planet.

Stay calm and rational. Make better decisions.

THE MAGIC OF ENTREPRENEURSHIP
Demonstrated by the street vendors in Rome

What entrepreneurs do best is identify an opportunity and respond to it. They observe the market, test customer response and then deliver what works at the right time and place.

As a tourist in Rome a few years ago, I noticed that the street vendors had almost all decided that the thousands of meandering tourists were most in need of either bottled water or a selfie-stick. Those were apparently the best-selling impulse items and they were offered everywhere. I did appreciate the water bottles during long tours of the ancient ruins in the hot sun, but was already hating the forest of selfie-sticks that were invading all my carefully composed souvenir photos and did not want to join in the contest of who could get their cell phone out in front of everyone else.

The street vendor sales strategy was simple and effective. A quick assessment of the passing prospects, a polite query then a quick decision to sell or move on to the next prospect. No time wasted on harassment or an obnoxious sales pitch. Pricing was competitive, one Euro for a bottle of water where the vendor was one of many and had a large stockpile and two Euros if he was alone in a remote corner with limited stock. The vendors also knew they were competing with bottles refilled from available public drinking fountains at no cost, so they all sold clearly branded and sealed bottled water that was ice cold.

But most impressive was their quick response to an unexpected thunderstorm and downpour chasing the tourists under cover. Like magic, suddenly all the street vendors were offering small collapsible umbrellas and cheap plastic rain ponchos! Quality and price were not an issue, we needed them here and now, so sales were brisk for those that had them.

Demonstrating effective sales tactics for entrepreneurs, whether you are a street vendor, a technology guru or the owner of a small business.

Be ready to respond to your market, rain or shine.

EVOLUTION OF DO-IT-YOURSELF MARKETING

Don't do it all yourself

It struck me recently in a meeting with two young entrepreneurs who were struggling to do their Web marketing all by themselves that we should instead be calling on professionals, who actually have the relevant expertise to get the best results for the minimum cost. Especially in social media marketing.

It looks easy, but it's not

We're all busy Tweeting, Facebook and Instagram posting and connecting on LinkedIn, thinking we know what we're doing. It all seems a necessary and obvious part of our marketing programs. But are we accomplishing anything? Raising awareness, building our brand, attracting prospects and future customers? Maybe not.

Much like running a restaurant or retail store, consumers recognize good versus bad performance, but that does not mean they know how to succeed at it themselves. It's never as easy as the experienced professionals make it look. It's usually better to pay for the advice to get it right the first time, instead of learning from the painful and expensive mistakes that may result from doing it ourselves.

We've been making the same mistakes in do-it-yourself marketing for decades.

Back in the 1980s, it was fun to play with all the available fonts and graphics in the new desktop software and then blast away with junk faxes. Not so much fun to discover that clients soon went from being impressed to being annoyed. Not the reaction we were going for. But we repeated the mistakes with junk e-mail. (Because it worked.) Eventually, we learned to be more respectful of inboxes and social media connections in order to build and retain customer loyalty and engagement.

We have done the same with other marketing initiatives, trying to imitate the best. It looks easy, but it's not. Choosing a brand name, slogan, graphics design, writing copy on websites and brochures. It all seems acceptable to the entrepreneur, until an experienced professional points out the lack of a clear, consistent marketing message directed at a well-defined target market and customer.

Use the professionals well, help them help you

Don't make the classic mistake of the entrepreneur who prefers to do it himself badly, rather than pay for an expensive professional.

Entrepreneurs by nature are curious and self-confident and will certainly try it on their own. Just remember to stop when you have learned enough to be a better, more knowledgeable client, so that you can direct the experts to get the results you want within the budget you can afford.

Try it yourself, learn the basics and then get good advice on how to do it better.

BRAGGING WORKS

If you've earned the right to brag

It worked for me running marathons. Long after my rational brain and aching body were telling me to quit, my ego kept reminding me that I would lose all bragging rights, if I didn't finish.

I knew it was much more satisfying to work into the conversation, "Yup, the full twenty-six miles, 42.2 kilometers and I wasn't last. In New York there were even nine thousand runners finished behind me!" (No need to mention there were twenty-five thousand ahead of me. Just a humble telling of the facts that put me in the best light. Getting too boastful can lead to distressing put downs, like "Did you win?")

Pride is a great motivator.

No need to deny it; earn it and use it. Don't exaggerate and don't take credit where it's not your accomplishment, but if it's true, let the world know. Sometimes it's not clear why we're so proud, but if the feeling is there, share it. And if you are proud of your team, your family, your staff or your associates, it's worth sharing. Being recognized and appreciated is a great motivator for everyone.

What about the things we do that we're not so proud of? The question then is, "Would you do that if anybody knew?" The opposite of pride is shame and it's a good deterrent to bad behaviour if you imagine it being exposed. If you anticipate embarrassment, humiliation or loss of respect, then don't do it.

Imagining an audience works both ways. Keep in mind that you may not be just imagining it. In today's over-exposed world somebody will notice, whatever you do.

EVERY BUSINESS IS A SOCIAL ENTERPRISE
It's an evolution of the community

The term "social enterprise" is starting to get annoying. Over-worked jargon used to make entrepreneurship in general, or a particular business seeking support, appear more appealing and acceptable to a cynical public that sees every business as evil and driven by the sole objective of making money for the senior executives and the shareholders.

Often the promoters of social entrepreneurship come across as "holier than thou," suggesting "I'm a good person and you're not, you filthy capitalist." Maybe I'm being too cynical, but let's dig a little deeper before giving one entrepreneur more credit than another for being socially responsible. Attaching a label does not answer all the questions.

Let's define a social enterprise as one whose primary objective is to address social issues. It can still be a sustainable and profitable business. And there is every reason to be optimistic that entrepreneurs can apply their skills in leadership, management and innovation to deliver effective solutions to social problems.

Is every charitable organisation or non-profit effective as a social enterprise? No. Some are corrupt, some are incompetent. Some pay their executives more than any profit-oriented enterprise could justify.

So their positive impact on society and social issues is actually less than the enlightened business that recognizes and respects its responsibilities to its employees, customers, suppliers, strategic partners, its community and the planet and acts accordingly.

Is every profit-oriented business an evil enterprise creating social problems? No, not all. Some are greedy, selfish or incompetent and they do exploit employees, customers, suppliers, strategic partners, their communities and the planet. They will not last.

The future will be better with both social enterprises and enlightened entrepreneurs. Let's speed up the process of natural selection, by supporting those that meet the criteria of having a positive impact on society.

Let the others go extinct.

TRUMP ELECTION LESSONS FOR YOUR BUSINESS

Democracy makes for bad decisions?

The election of Donald Trump in 2016 was a shock and a disappointment to many of us. The political analysts and commentators, both experts and amateurs, have debated it intensely for years and will analyse and try to explain it for decades.

But what have we learned from it that might be applicable to our businesses?

Here are some discussion points that I suggest you can share with your management team, the next time they stray off the topic and insist on talking about politics, instead of the business issues of the day.

1. Democracy does not always deliver the results you expect or want.

2. Be careful of the limited choices that you offer.

3. The most popular choice is often not the best choice.

4. Leadership needs to listen. But empathy is not enough. Without an effective response to the complaints, you will be labelled as weak and ineffective and risk being replaced.

5. Stop talking to, and listening to, only the people who agree with you.

6. Stop assuming that you can persuade people by logical arguments. Do not write them off as ignorant or irrational. Recognize they are just influenced differently from you.

7. You cannot persuade your opponents to change by using the influencers and channels of communication that they do not trust.

8. The reasons for making a particular choice are volatile, unpredictable and not always subject to explanation or analysis, by the experts or the voters themselves, before or after the fact.

9. Plato said it first: "Beware of democracy: ordinary people are too easily influenced by the emotional and deceptive rhetoric of ambitious politicians."

10. Effective leadership has a responsibility to make difficult decisions, explain them satisfactorily, implement them effectively and ensure that any negative consequences are adequately addressed.

Winston Churchill graciously defended democracy, after losing his bid for re-election in July of 1945, as follows, "Democracy is the worst form of government, except for all those other forms that have been tried from time to time."

He may have been right about government and we should all exercise our democratic right to vote and defend and protect our democratic institutions.

But in your business, good management is a better idea than taking a vote.

BACK TO SCHOOL

Not just for kids

After the summer vacations, it's time for back to school. But once the kids are settled in, it's also a good time for you and your team to go back to school and learn more about how to do better for yourselves and your business. Expand your knowledge or take a refresher course in the fundamentals for better personal and business performance.

You've probably already established your preferred sources for ideas and inspiration, but consider expanding your horizons, dig a little deeper, try something new.

Go beyond scanning the Tweets and posts on Facebook or LinkedIn. Read your favourite guru's latest book, or try somebody completely different. Take a course, hire a coach or go to a conference or seminar outside your industry or profession. Take up yoga or music lessons. Maybe learn more about sociology, economics, political history or comparative religions to better understand what is going on in the world around us.

Share what you learn or coax others through the personal development process. Become the teacher and be surprised by how much better you will understand the subject yourself.

Feel like a kid again, go back to school.

WHO ARE YOU LISTENING TO? WHY?

Only very smart people. Because they agree with me.

But are you learning anything new?

Do they make you think or act differently?

That's the best way to tell if you learned anything.

It doesn't seem to matter which mainstream news source we read, watch or listen to, they all seem to agree on what is important to us and what we should be angry about. Then they insist on pushing the same story and analysis, over and over for days, with too much mind-numbing repetitiveness.

Whether it's current affairs, politics, sports or business, it's hard work to dig deeper and get the whole story or find any thoughtful and perceptive analysis that goes beyond the initial impressions. But we need to do it, if we really want to have things change.

We need to be less passive and more selective in where we go for news, information and analysis. That means avoiding the easy choice of following those sources and analysts that we agree with or we have something in common with.

It also requires making an effort to listen to people whom we don't like or don't agree with and avoid simply dismissing them as ignorant or evil. That's not easy either. Especially when the tactic is so widely used to effectively stop discussion.

Remember: *The Seven Habits of Highly Effective People* by Stephen Covey includes, "Seek first to understand before seeking to be understood." That is a much better process for seeking compromise and achieving agreed solutions.

Keep on the path for knowledge and wisdom and continue to learn, make changes and make a difference.

(And thank you for including me among your learning resources.)

MANAGE LIKE A HOCKEY MOM

But in a good way

Hockey games are always exciting and entertaining, whether it's the NHL or kids in minor hockey and they often provide inspiration and ideas applicable beyond the hockey rink.

At a grandson's Peewee hockey tournament in Montreal, the welcome brochure included the Quebec Hockey Association's **Code of Ethics for Parents** (also useful for grandparents) to encourage responsible behaviour and allow both players and their parents to simply enjoy the game.

In reading it, I realized it could be adapted as a useful guide for business owners and managers. Here is my adaptation.

The Code of Ethics for Entrepreneurs

As a business owner and responsible manager, I recognize that I have the potential and the opportunity to make an important contribution to the personal development and well-being of the individuals who choose to work with me and I accept that as a priority over "winning the game."

I will therefore ensure my conduct continually demonstrates the following principles:

1. *I understand that my employees are here for their benefit and pleasure, not mine.*

2. *I consider winning as part of the pleasure of playing the game; I will not exaggerate the pain of failure; and I will recognize errors as a necessary part of the learning experience.*

3. *I will respect the efforts and the decisions of the supporters and supervisors and of the outside authorities responsible for enforcing the rules and regulations. I will do my best to understand and accept the rules and regulations applicable to my business.*

4. *I will recognize and respect good performance on the part of any individual employee, as well as that of the individuals on competing teams.*

5. *I accept each individual's limitations and will not project my own ambitions or unreasonable expectations upon anyone. My expectations will be appropriate to the qualifications and capabilities of each individual.*

6. *I will demonstrate and expect from all employees a reflection of the important values of respect, discipline, effort and loyalty.*

7. *I will not encourage or tolerate any level of inter-personal harassment, conflict or aggressive behavior.*

8. *I will encourage and support the personal development of skills and capabilities for every individual.*

Good advice from responsible hockey moms.

(I do notice that a lot gets ignored during the playoffs when winning is everything, but that's another issue for a future article. Meanwhile, the hockey analysts are all over it.)

Be better. Do better.

As a responsible hockey parent and as an enlightened entrepreneur.

STRATEGIC CHOICES: PORSCHE OR PICK-UP TRUCK?

Focus and forget pleasing everybody.

Whatever business issue or challenge you're facing, I believe you should always start from a strategic perspective. Step back, way back, and ask yourself if the solution you're considering is consistent with your strategic plan and will move you toward your long-term objectives.

Have you made explicit strategic choices and communicated them effectively to your employees and your customers? Or are you too busy with operational issues and management challenges to think strategically. Often the strategy has just evolved organically as you respond to changes in the business environment, the competition and customer preferences. Perhaps it's time to assess where you are strategically and decide if that's where you want to be.

In order to clarify a company's strategic positioning, branding and corporate personality, my colleague Lp Camozzi and I used to ask clients the question, "If your business were an automobile, what would it be?"

Confusion and contradiction were often evident. And even more revealing was to compare the owner's answer to the automobile suggested by managers, sales staff and customers. The owner thinks Porsche and the customers think pick-up truck? We have a problem.

For better strategic focus and improved results in the market, clarity and consistency are important. First determine the characteristics, features, and performance of the automobile you would prefer for your corporate role model. Then maintain that strategic focus and ensure consistent communication of the key elements in all your internal and external messaging.

And forget about being the first to design and build a Porsche-Pickup that is sporty and luxurious, can carry a load of bricks and pull a horse trailer. Pick one and focus!

Remember that the camel started out as a race horse, designed by a committee to please everybody and the result was an ugly miserable failure (unless you need to travel long distances in the desert).

HAVING A BAD DAY?

Don't expect so much. Be grateful for what you've got.

After one more setback it's easy to slide down the road of regrets.

"If only…." "I should have, could have…." "How did I get here?"

"Is this all there is?" "I'm working hard, why am I not rich and famous yet?" "My best years are behind me." "It's too late now."

That thinking will not help. Time to change your mindset.

Instead of moaning and groaning and dreaming of what might have been, take a look at what you have to be thankful for.

Think of the people who have real concerns and complaints in their lives. Imagine the millions around the world who are much worse off than you.

Do you deserve your good fortune? Did you earn it?

A little humility and gratitude will get you started on a better road. Be happy with what you have, instead of unhappy with what you do not have. Start by indulging in some spontaneous kindness or a generous gift to the unfortunate. Then go with the glow of feeling good about yourself.

The world will be a better place. And you will be a better person in it.

Be better.

CHASING THE BIG DEAL

Small deals may be a better idea

When you know that increasing sales will solve your problems, it is tempting to chase the one big deal that will solve them all quickly.

It could be a mistake. Maybe it's better to say, "No thanks for now."

It can be great for your ego and your brand if you win a big deal and make the headlines. But it may be only a short-term win based on a small price difference, recent product improvement or service innovation. You may be only a temporary choice as a negotiating tactic between the customer and their regular supplier. Don't get too comfortable. The big guys who lost the order will not leave you alone for long and they will not make it easier next time.

Winning that big deal can solve some problems, but it may introduce new ones. Do you have the resources and financing to deliver as promised? Will you now be too dependent on one big customer? Will your other customers be concerned, disappointed or feel neglected and start to leave? Have all the risks been considered?

Before even making a presentation or proposal on that tempting big deal, be sure to check that it fits with your strategic plan. Are you matching your competitive strengths to a clear long-term opportunity? Or are you *swinging and hoping?* Will you be able to build on this success or are you making an all-or-nothing bet?

Building your business slowly but continuously, one customer at a time and one deal at a time will make you a stronger competitor and more likely to become the next big guy doing the next big deal.

ANNOYING DISTURBANCES

To Prevent, Avoid or Ignore?

A pleasant walk in the sunshine this morning was interrupted first by the dive-bombing red-winged blackbirds along the riverside, then by the swarms of annoying mosquitoes in the woods.

Back at the office it may continue. The noisy air-conditioning, your neighbour listening to the ranting talk radio show or the constant interruptions by telemarketers.

You only have three choices in dealing with annoying disturbances:
- Prevent
- Avoid
- Ignore

And they may not all be available to you.

They easiest and most obvious reaction to the annoying distraction may not be the best long-term solution. Cursing and swatting at the blackbirds and mosquitoes didn't seem to help.

But if your productivity, performance or enjoyment are being adversely affected, it's worth recognizing that ignoring the annoying disturbances is not working.

Try the prevent or avoid solution.

MAKE WORK FUN

A simple principle for good management

Make work fun. It really is that simple. Don't make it more complicated.

I know, it's more complicated!

But let's try to reduce good management down to one simple guiding principle.

Your job as a manager is to ensure that your employees are working effectively to meet the department's and the company's objectives. That requires that individual objectives must be aligned with the objectives of the business.

Having more fun is one objective that we can all agree on. Especially if we accept that making money is fun! For both the employee and the business.

Don't make it more complicated.

Take a look at what you have to change or fix, so that work is more fun. Provide leadership, remove obstacles, give recognition. Everything else will take care of itself. Your staff will get the job done and meet their objectives. And you will meet yours.

All the while, everybody is having fun.

See, it really is that simple.

CONSTRUCTIVE, NOT CRITICISM
Please, no useless commentary.

"Whoa, that didn't work out as planned."

Thanks, but I already knew that.

If you are going to comment on my performance, please take the time to suggest something helpful. Don't just pile on with more useless criticism. All that does is kill my enthusiasm to try harder and do better next time.

Every performance review will be more constructive if it starts with the positive. "The packaging looks good." "The price is very competitive." "Well, at least nobody died."

Followed by the helpful suggestion, **"and it would be even better, if…."** Not followed by, **"but you really screwed up this time …."**

Decide before you speak: Is this a complaint, a useless observation or a constructive suggestion? If you don't do it yourself, then you cannot expect it from your critics.

If they still don't get it, I find it helpful to conclude the discussion with, *"Thank you for your input. Please don't take it personally, if I choose to ignore it."*

MODERN MANAGERS ARE SMARTER

Are you?

Remember the bad old days when managers judged performance by all the wrong indicators? The managing partner who questions whether a consultant is ready for promotion because, "I'm not sure of his commitment to the firm. I never see him taking his briefcase home at night." Not noticing that the same consultant was usually going home after six and had built a roster of very satisfied clients. Or the ambitious manager promoting himself by denigrating a colleague for arriving late to his staff meeting, ignoring the fact he was the same individual willing to forego family obligations to attend corporate events on evenings and weekends.

Modern managers are more likely to look at real performance, not superficial appearances, individual work habits or personality traits. Judging and rewarding for results, not effort and time spent at the office. Enabling work-life balance and accommodating family needs to improve employee satisfaction.

I recommend a very enlightening book on the subject of managing performance, *First, Break all the Rules* (© 1999), by Marcus Buckingham and Curt Coffman, based on their study of high performance managers and how they succeed. The essential theme is that those managers ignore company rules and standard policies to treat everyone differently according to their needs. Don't try to change who they are and how they work, find out what they like to do and are good at, then let them do it their way.

Modern managers do not follow the lead of their rule-bound old-fashioned predecessors.

Are you a modern manager?

TIMING IS EVERYTHING

And it's your choice

In decision making, we often spend a lot of time analyzing who, what, where and why, without giving sufficient consideration to when. It seems obvious, let's do it as soon as possible, now that we've decided. But maybe not.

We always have a choice to make. It's now or later. Maybe never. Deciding not to decide is also a choice. But when to go or not go is the real question.

We cannot go backwards and do it sooner than right now, so let's not waste time on regrets and the shoulda, woulda, coulda self-flagellation. Your choice of timing may have more impact on the consequences than all the other considerations. It's an important decision: When?

Whether it's to start-up or shut down, launch or terminate, hire or fire, buy or sell. Timing may be more important to getting the best results than any of the other decisions. The discussions and decisions on packaging, pricing, target markets, marketing copy, graphics design, sales pitches, tools and tactics may never end. You can always wait for more information, lower costs, better test results, or more resources.

It's your choice and you'll be wrong a lot of the time. Remember not to waste time on looking back and beating yourself up. Extract the lessons you can from the learning experience and do better next time.

SUMMER JOBS

What did *you* learn?

It's time to get back to school soon and the kids are enjoying the last few days of their summer jobs. Remember those days yourself? Fun in the sun, hanging out with friends, pool parties, BBQ and beer. Working on your sun tan and hitting on the other cute kids. Is that what you remember?

But it was not all fun. It was a job and it may have involved garbage collection, cleaning toilets, digging ditches, mowing lawns, making beds, hauling heavy loads or serving hostile customers. All while avoiding boredom, exhaustion and a demanding and difficult boss.

But there were important life lessons learned. Simple lessons, but important ones:

- Show up on time, work hard.
- Focus on the task at hand.
- Be responsible for your actions.
- Pay attention to the customer, the boss and the environment – in that order.
- Use the right tool for the right job, be aware of safety and security issues.
- Get your priorities straight – work, personal, family and social.
- Better performance leads to better jobs.
- Save your money.

Let's hope the kids today are learning those lessons too. They will be better employees, bosses and entrepreneurs, if they learn from their summer jobs.

THE BLAME GAME

Goddamn the …?

My dad grew up on a farm in Saskatchewan where the most hated company in the country was the CPR, responsible for railway service across the prairies.

Dad liked to tell the story of the angry farmer who complained, "I lost my crop in a hail storm, my truck broke down, my dog died and my wife left me. Goddamn the CPR!"

Quebec politicians for decades explained their every failure, "*c'est la faute du fédéral!*" It was always Ottawa's fault.

We all have lots of scapegoats available to us every day. For every failure, foul-up, screw-up, disaster or disappointment, choose your favourite. Blame the oil companies, the media, or Donald Trump. Evil rich white guys. Google or Microsoft. It's a long list if you try.

But the blame game is too easy and it gets us nowhere. Just a lazy way to end the conversation and stop doing anything to tackle the issue. *It's not my fault and there's nothing I can do.*

Let's stop looking for who to blame.

Let's look harder for who can fix it and how we can help.

THE PRICE IS THE PRICE – ALMOST NEVER

And it's a problem. Preoccupation with price leads to bad decisions, if we miss the important factors that determine value.

We have all seen frequent examples of nonsensical pricing and have our own favourite stories of a deal we have boasted about, without admitting that it turned out badly. TV ads. Only $19.95! Buy now and get another one for free, with a bonus carrying case, and free shipping. *Beware of side effects. Certain conditions apply.* What could go wrong for only $19.95?

Last weekend I bought three new sweaters at the Tommy Hilfiger store for only $19.99 each. Regularly $84.99! (The sales clerk admitted they never sell anything in the store at the "regular" price.)

My favourite example was during a guided tour in Tangiers that led us to a local carpet manufacturer. Beautiful handmade carpet, "retails in America for $2500, factory price only $700!" We negotiated them down to $200. *Wow, what a deal.* Then on the way back to the tour bus, we met a street vendor with what appeared to be exactly the same carpet for only $100. We said "no thanks," until he followed us onto the tour bus and eventually came down to $20. Now we can boast of two matching carpets for only $220. But I wonder, were they really handmade and high quality? Was the second one stolen?

And that's the problem with focusing on the price. Consumers insist on it, but usually fail to ask why the price is so low. Is it cost reduced to the point of being unsafe and unreliable? Was it manufactured in a dangerous, environment-destroying factory using child labour? Who cares, look at the price!

It may be the seller's strategy, to attract or distract with the price. But buyer beware, there is always more than the price to consider before you decide to buy.

P.S. Did you notice this book sells for only $19.95? Sometimes less!

THE PEOPLE PROBLEM

The challenge of making good fits

A recent conversation with an entrepreneur drawn unexpectedly into a family business, reminded me that the biggest challenge to building and growing a better business is managing the relationships within the organisation.

Like him and most other entrepreneurs I know, you may be confident and competent in the primary domain essential to the business — technology, operations, financial management or sales and marketing. But managing people and inter-personal relationships is a tougher challenge. And it can be painful to be continuously drawn into issues that you are not interested in and not good at. You would rather focus on other priorities and ignore the distractions of performance reviews, compensation and benefit plans, managers that are competing instead of co-operating, conflict between employees on the job, petty complaints about policy and procedures, questions about who is doing what and why.

People do make it challenging and maybe you can delegate to a human resource professional, but as the owner/manager you have to ensure that people and relationship issues are not holding back business performance.

The solution lies in making good fits. Getting the right people in the right jobs, doing what they are both good at and like to do. Building teams at all levels that deliver better performance and solutions because they communicate well and effectively share their different strengths, knowledge and experience.

It starts with open two-way communication throughout the organisation. From the corporate mission statement, strategy and objectives down to the choice of furnishings at the reception desk.

Advise, listen, explain. Listen again, explain again. People will still be a challenge, but they're too important to your success to be neglected.

EVIL GREEDY ENTREPRENEURS
Reinforcing the stereotypes

There is always a lot of angry rhetoric around any government proposals that favour small business. "Trying to encourage small business owners who are the engine of economic growth and prosperity for the whole country," is their usual explanation. "Removing tax loop-holes that only favour the big corporations."

But the policy debate quickly deteriorates into complaints of the evil greedy entrepreneur ripping off the exploited middle-class wage slave. Critics of the proposed reforms react with their own stereotypes of corrupt politicians and powerful company CEOs and billionaires buying influence.

Unfortunately, too much of the raging rhetoric just reinforces the stereotypes.

Dealing with real problems is complicated and needs more than a political quick fix. The politicians are right when they say it isn't easy, but that's no excuse for doing it badly. A poorly conceived and poorly communicated tax reform package does not help improve the fairness of the system or the understanding of required changes.

If we can be more tolerant and understanding in other cases of biased stereotyping, "Of course, they're not all like that," then why not for politicians, bureaucrats and business people. They're not all driven by ignorance, prejudice and self-interest.

IT TAKES A CONVERSATION
Not a lecture

"What we've got here is a failure to communicate," followed by the evil warden delivering a severe beating to drive the message into the dumb prisoner's thick skull. Maybe it works in the movies.

But the approach is probably as useless as raising the volume or relentlessly repeating the same message. If you do not have engagement with your audience, the message will not resonate. They may seem receptive, even enthusiastic, but nothing changes unless you get commitment to the objectives, the plan and the expected action for each participant.

Don't lecture to a passive listener. You're wasting everybody's time. Nodding and taking notes may be a positive sign, but it's not enough. You need personal commitment.

Yes, I understand. Yes, I will do that.

Start a conversation. Ask questions and listen attentively yourself. Adapt your pitch, presentation or plan and check if they really understand. What are they going to do differently? What are you going to do differently, now that you have their input? When and how?

Two-way communication is always better than a lecture, if you really want to change behavior and improve performance.

Even if you only want to inform, advise or inspire. Feedback and comments start the conversation and help people understand each other better.

NO CONFLICT OF INTEREST?

Look closer

The next time an agent, broker, lawyer or advisor offers to help by working on both sides of the deal, say "No thanks."

If they try to tell you there is no conflict of interest for them, then reply, "Either you know you're lying or you do not. Either way, I'm disappointed. And the answer is still, no thanks."

They see no conflict of interest because their only interest is maximizing their own return on the deal. Sorry, but there is no other way to explain it.

They may try to sell the concept of mutual interests and you may get all parties including the advisors, to agree on a deal, but compromises will be made that were not necessary and may only please the dealmakers.

Aligning mutual interests, or the naively optimistic cliché of "win/ win" may sound easy and look obvious.

It's not.

DISASTER INSURANCE

Reducing risks

Strange concept, insurance. You hope a disaster never happens, but you expect that it will someday, so you buy insurance to recover when it does. The insurance company takes your money, also hoping it never happens. If it does happen you win (at least on the insurance) and they lose.

Flood, fire or theft, commercial liability, death or disability. You can insure against any of those disasters, and you probably should, but how much coverage should you pay for and what risks should you accept?

The insurance company has the advantage of knowing more than you do and pricing their insurance accordingly. They're able to pool a large number of clients with the same risk and can more precisely calculate the odds of paying out. Your choice is to not buy insurance and accept both the risk of the disaster and the potential consequences. Maybe you can recover from the disaster with the money you saved on insurance premiums. Probably not a good bet. But don't buy more insurance than you need. That's good for insurance company profits, not yours.

You can, of course, reduce the risks and the costs by taking preventive measures. Quitting smoking and avoiding sky diving will reduce both the life insurance premiums and the risk of premature death.

What about business risks? Same concept.

Reduce the risk of disaster and the potential consequences by maintaining adequate security systems, signing long-term contracts with major customers and suppliers and confidentiality agreements with key employees, have appropriate insurance coverage for business interruption and commercial liabilities, meet regulatory and environmental requirements, hedge foreign exchange and receivables risks and prepare contingency plans for potential surprises.

Review the risk management checklist for your specific business and see if you should do more.

Don't wait until the fires are close enough that you can smell the smoke.

YOU'RE FIRED!

Hire well, but fire better

Donald Trump made his name as a Reality TV star with the trademark line, "You're fired!" As President in the real world, instead of the very unreal Reality TV world, he may have used it too many times. People have learned that he demands unquestioning loyalty, but offers none himself.

There is a lesson here for entrepreneurs. Firing an employee needs to be done at least as well as the initial hiring, maybe better. A firing has greater immediate impact on the rest of the organisation. Although your conversations one-on-one with a departing employee may be very private, a firing tends to get more attention and generate stronger reaction. Maybe it's the "fear of firing."

The message received by employees staying on the job may be more important than the message delivered to the employee who was fired. Their perceptions and interpretations of what really happened will affect their own behavior.

They have seen how someone got fired, now they need to know why. Could it just be something the boss suddenly didn't like? Something that was said or done that had nothing to do with the job? Be sure they get the right message, quickly.

Everybody's watching.

Even if you're not on reality TV.

PARTICIPATIVE MANAGEMENT – YOU CANNOT FAKE IT.

Is your business run democratically? Probably not.

Employees do not get to vote, managers are supposed to be responsible and make consistently good decisions. Let's not confuse them with too many contrary, ill-informed opinions. We have seen too many unhappy conclusions from democratic decision-making lately.

It is easier to accept your role as the lonely leader and try to be the gentle and wise, all-knowing autocratic decision-maker. "I am the owner, so I get to decide." That's true, but you will make even better decisions with relevant input from the troops.

It's called participative management. It means soliciting input before decisions are made and plans are set. It means seeking feedback on current operations and on the results from new initiatives. It cannot be a token effort with input from others that is subsequently ignored. It needs to be sincere and must include setting realistic expectations and responding promptly to suggestions, questions and complaints.

You will find that early participation in new initiatives will help you develop better implementation plans that are mutually agreed and have the support and commitment of the people required to deliver the intended results.

Democracy is good.

But handle it carefully and manage it well.

"I KNEW THAT. I DO THAT"

Obviously

Sometimes when you're working on a self-improvement program or reading the latest business textbook, or following a self-help advice blog or podcast or participating in a workshop or seminar from your preferred expert, guru or philosopher king, you may suddenly think, "Hey, that's obvious. I already knew that. Of course I do that."

The experts agree, "I'm doing it right!"

But is that reassuring or disturbing?

Good to have your own ideas and approach confirmed? Or dammit, I paid too much to learn something I already knew? Does it build your confidence and conviction or seed new doubt and anxiety? Maybe you need to keep searching for better answers.

I'm recommending that you choose to find it reassuring, building confidence and conviction. You're smarter than you think. It's time to stop searching and researching. Don't let continuous learning and preparation become an excuse for procrastination. Get to work and make the changes.

But keep learning by doing. Keep developing and adapting your ideas and approach to your own circumstances and capabilities. Nobody knows the possibilities for constant improvement better than you do.

HIDING IN ANONYMITY

Who me?

Bad behaviour is easier when it's anonymous. As you've already noticed, I'm sure.

In traffic behind tinted windows in a closed car, drivers are more likely to be rude, selfish and inconsiderate. Online, aggressive and inappropriate behaviour is even worse and made easier if it's anonymous.

Some people enjoy the attention and notoriety of their Twitter tirades and posted rants, but for the most egregious, we don't usually know exactly who it is or where they live.

So how do we raise standards of social behaviour and civil discourse?

Maybe it starts with not allowing anyone to hide behind anonymity. If they were required to disclose their names and let us see their faces, they would be less likely to embarrass themselves. More likely to say and do things they can be proud of. Boasting is better than ranting, tell us who you are and where you work.

Think about it the next time you recognize that you are hiding in anonymity. Be proud.

Better yet, make us all proud to be among your friends and associates. Tell us your name.

LONELY AT THE TOP

It doesn't have to be

You could be proud of the fact that you are all alone running your business. Or you could be constantly complaining and feeling sorry for yourself. Or you can make different choices.

It can be lonely at the top, but it doesn't have to be.

Sharing your challenges and looking for solutions by confiding in family, friends or employees may not be enough. In fact, some of the issues may be caused by family, friends and employees and you've already learned that sharing with them is not always helpful. You need knowledgeable, experienced, objective input from outside that inner circle. You cannot possibly consider all the viable options and develop the best solutions in isolation.

So how do you expand your circle of confidants to break the cycle of struggling alone looking for better answers? Consider these options, which can work well for independent business owners:

- Use professional advisors – your accountant, lawyer or business consultant.
- Hire a mentor or personal coach.
- Recruit an advisory board.
- Join a peer advisory group of similar, but non-competing, independent business owners.
- Seek advice from trusted strategic partners – your banker, customer, supplier, even a co-operative competitor.

You do not have to be alone at the top.

UNDER PROMISE & OVER DELIVER, BUT –

Don't Under Sell

It's a popular mantra: *Under Promise & Over Deliver*

And it's good advice for achieving consistently high levels of customer satisfaction. Promise delivery in the next 3 to 5 days, then deliver tomorrow. Wow!

Customers love it. Except those customers who did not order it, because they needed it in two days.

Cautious promises may be good for customer service, but not good for sales to get the order in the first place. It's never a good idea to promise more than you can deliver, but maybe you just need to try harder to give customers what they want when they want it.

Maybe the mantra should be:
Better than you expect. Let me surprise you.

IT'S ALL ABOUT THE MONEY

Of course

As they keep telling us, "It's always about the money."

Maybe we should accept the truth? Stop denying, explaining or apologizing? Maybe we can just ignore the critics and carry on making money.

Unfortunately, the critics can influence the environment you work in and the rules you have to comply with, even if they don't know what they're talking about.

So let's help them understand what entrepreneurs are really about. Don't let them accept all the easy stereotypes and generalize from the few bad actors. We could use a little more sympathy and understanding. Running a business is not as simple as it looks.

We already know that we could make more money, especially in the short term, by taking a few short cuts. They're not all illegal, some are just objectionably exploitive of people and the planet. But we also know that they are actually bad for business. If we want to build and grow a viable long-term business we must take care of the people, the communities and the environment where we work. They are all important to us.

We don't need to apologize (I hope), but we do need to explain that we understand the critics and we're trying to do better, for all of us.

Be better. Do better.

BREAKFAST STRATEGIES

Just two scrambled eggs, bacon, coffee, toast & jam, please.

And, as my dad used to say, "On the double with a smile."

I spend a lot of time in restaurants having breakfast with entrepreneurs, colleagues and associates. Observing the variety of breakfast spots and their business models has been a useful lesson in strategic positioning. The specialty breakfast restaurant is a well-established concept, especially in Montréal, and is a very competitive market with lots of attractive choices. How do they all survive?

Here's what I've learned, after extensive "market research".

First: Accept the business model where it's clearly working.

Breakfast and lunch only, located in a high traffic area for large volume and fast turnover during limited working hours. Appeal to the most likely prospects, business people, professionals or retirees, dining alone or using the restaurant for business meetings and socializing in the real world.

Second: Be distinctive.

Make deliberate choices on the menu, pricing, quality and quantity, design and décor, staffing, uniforms, style and personality. Be consistent in all of those choices to reinforce the strategic positioning.

A restaurant can choose to emulate MacDonald's or Tim Horton's style of high volume with limited choices, delivered fast and cheap. Or consider more variety, larger selections, larger portions, more creative menu items, gourmand or gourmet, extravagant or exotic, homestyle or fancy cuisine. Always ensuring attention to high quality and friendly, efficient service.

It's a simple formula for success:
Make good strategic choices;
Be consistent in execution of the strategy.

It works for more than restaurants. The research continues.

RETAIL IS DEAD

Hah! They said that about the horse & buggy industry.

We've been saying it about retail for decades.

"E-commerce is coming, catch the wave or be drowned by it!"

Soon there will be nobody left but Amazon for everything. Every holiday shopping season we predict the final slide into oblivion for traditional real-world retailers. And we're wrong again.

Resilient retailers keep surprising us. They're not all losing to online. Yes, we've seen the disturbing sight of Sear's liquidation sales at one end of the mall, but BestBuy and Staples seem busy and full of real shoppers.

Survival of the fittest still applies. The laggards at the back of the pack will get picked off by the predators. You can't hide from the online competitors, but you don't have to roll over and die, either. Evolution and survival requires adaptation.

Pay attention. Learn from new competitors and their business models, online or otherwise. Copy what seems to be working to attract and retain your customers too.

The latest versions of the new economy may include robots and artificial intelligence, drones and data mining, but some old rules still apply:

- Do your homework before trying to implement new technology.
- Focus on your business objectives, not on what's cool, or hot, or trendy.
- Do not stubbornly fail to fix what is clearly broken.
- Integrate online and offline – for storefronts, product presentation, customer service and order fulfillment.
- Measure, monitor and manage performance.

- Review, reload and fire again.

Too many new initiatives are still driven by fear of losing to the competition or missing a short-term fad. Don't be complacent or over confident, but don't be impatient or impulsive either.

Be smarter than that. You're not dead yet.

PRICING TO PLEASE

Not everybody, just your target customers

"Can you do better?"

Back when I was selling computer hardware to resellers in Boston that was the usual response when I quoted a price. Actually, in Boston it was more like, "Can yuh do bettah?"

My smart-ass reply was often, "Better for you or for me?" Isn't that the question? But that makes it a win-lose proposition, instead of a mutually beneficial transaction. What price will satisfy both the buyer and the seller? That's the real question.

Buyers want a price that compares favourably to their alternatives and delivers value to their business. Sellers want a price that exceeds their cost and delivers sufficient volume to be profitable to their business. An acceptable price is defined by your potential customer's prior experience with the competition.

The right price is a key strategic decision and must be consistent with your own choices for product quality, features, benefits and associated services. Price is an important element in your market positioning.

Do you want the price to be the primary reason customers are attracted to your business?

Or is your product more unique than that and your customer more discriminating. If you win on price, you can also easily lose on price. Long-term loyal relationships are built on a consistently positive customer experience that confirms your integrity, expertise and business values. Price and availability are only the initial entry criteria.

You cannot please everybody, so use pricing to help select the customers you really want to do business with.

THE POWER OF NO

Be willing to walk away.

It's not a tactic and it's not a bluff.

It's a change in attitude that changes the relationship
for both sides.

Now you're only here because you both want to be.

And you're working toward the same objective.

Confronted with a potential no, both parties will find
a better way to get to the win-win.

Or agree to walk away to consider other options.

Stop wasting each other's time.

LEAD BY EXAMPLE

Show the way and how to behave getting there

Leadership means more than showing the way to achieve your goals and improve group performance. It requires demonstrating your guiding principles in dealing with the inevitable challenges in working with colleagues, associates, customers and business partners.

People are more likely to be persuaded by your example than by your rhetoric. Strong language and loud words are not more persuasive. Leadership by command and control may still work, but not as well as leading by example.

Leading by example means more than "Look at me, I'm rich and famous. You can be too." Yes, bullying and self-promotion may get you there, even get you elected as President of the most powerful and influential country in the world. But you will not remain in charge for long. People will resist. They will make it difficult, maybe cause you to fail. You will never receive the respect and have the influence that you seek if you abuse the power of your leadership role.

It's better to demonstrate good character and higher moral standards of respect, compassion and kindness for those who struggle to obtain what you already enjoy.

Leadership that meets those standards will generate loyal followers and we can all be proud of what we achieve together.

Be better. Do better.

EXCEEDING EXPECTATIONS
Even if you're not working for tips

Good waiters and bartenders get it.

Prepare a good product.
Meet the minimum expectations for delivery,
quality and price.
Add a friendly personal touch.

Demonstrate your expertise and dispense your
worldly-wise advice. Create a more knowledgeable buyer,
who appreciates you.

It's good for tips.
Even better if you're not working for tips.

You'll win loyal customers and raving fans.

CUSTOMER SERVICE IS MARKETING?

Simply deliver what you promised

A recent Linkedin article argued that Customer Service is the New Marketing – do it right and traditional marketing is unnecessary.

I would argue that it's an essential element of a three part process – Marketing, Sales and Customer Service working together to meet the objectives of attracting, satisfying and keeping loyal, long-term profitable customers.

The three elements must be complementary and consistent to be effective. Promote what you can actually deliver. Do not under-sell it, but do not promise and hope that it can be delivered. Or that the customer will not notice the deficiencies. That never ends well.

The sales effort has to be part of the process after marketing has introduced the customers. Continue to qualify and confirm that you can meet their needs and desires while avoiding the easy sale by telling them whatever they want to hear. The truth is better, even if it's a disappointment for both of you.

Customer service simply makes sure that the promises are met with competence, helpful support and a friendly smile that says, "Y'all come back now." And they will.

HIGH PRESSURE SALES TACTICS

Because they work

If you've recently strolled near any resort hotel on a southern beach, then you've probably been introduced to the "body snatchers" – timeshare salesmen offering attractive incentives – free dinner, golf, Cirque de Soleil tickets – for you to attend a brief sales presentation at their resort.

It sounds good until you waste half a day being held hostage by a hierarchy of high pressure sales people persuading you to buy into the timeshare concept. It can turn into a very unpleasant vacation experience.

Or you can learn something useful from the experience to take home for your business. Here are my thoughts, after four weeks in Mexico listening to the pitches and the complaints.

For Sellers:

1. Train sales people well and ensure consistent use of the most effective tactics.

2. Remember that every question, problem or complaint can be resolved by selling a solution – an upgrade, another product, a new service package.

3. Keep all the initial prices high enough to allow for negotiated discounts and package deals and still leave room for generous buyer incentives and sales commissions.

4. Ensure sales reps are careful not to oversell or promise too much. Avoid the potential complaints of deliberately misleading claims or lying to prospects.

5. Build in a process for confirming and clarifying the terms and conditions to ensure customer understanding and acceptance before sign-off.

6. Ensure that operations and customer service staff have the same understanding of product and service offerings and can effectively resolve any "misunderstandings" that may persist.

7. Avoid the generally negative customer perceptions of high pressure sales tactics, but achieve the effectiveness of a focused, motivated, well-trained and well-managed sales force.

For Buyers:

1. Push past the prepared pitch and the recommended sales solution to every problem.

2. Gain control of the agenda and lead the sellers to your preferred solution, not theirs.

3. Get all your questions answered clearly before making any decisions.

4. Be as aggressive and persistent as the sellers are.

5. Get it in writing. Read it carefully before signing.

All basic principles that you already knew, reinforced by observing high-pressure timeshare sales tactics. Apply them to your own business when you get home, but without the negative side effects.

(Meanwhile, try to enjoy your winter vacations in the south in spite of the annoying sales tactics.)

GOOD SALESMANSHIP STILL WORKS

And you can't fake sincerity

Ambushed at the service counter. But it was such a smooth, subtle switch from the service welcome to the sales pitch that I was persuaded to sit down and listen.

As soon as I got out of the car at the dealership service bay, I noticed the well-dressed young man coming to greet me. He said, "Good morning, Mr. Chatterson, let me check you in right away to get your winter tires installed," as he handed me the service ticket. "Then I want to talk to you this morning about trading in your car. It has low mileage and good trade-in value and we have some exceptional deals right now that would make it easy for you to trade up to a new one."

How's that for a well delivered up-sell? Much more appealing than, "Would you like fries with that?" He handed me a cup of freshly brewed coffee and led me to his desk.

How could I resist. I'm an entrepreneur and sales guy, too. I was appreciating the demonstration of good salesmanship. He almost had me into a new convertible on a cold windy winter day in Montreal. The deal was very good!

But then he fell back on the objectionable old car dealer sales routine of, "Let me introduce you to the Sales Manager. He can do even better." He walked me over to a large private office to meet the manager. Older guy, more expensive suit, big hearty handshake, high energy, fast talker and, "Very pleased to meet you, Mr. Chatterson."

A forced fake friendliness that turned me off and sent me back to the service department for another coffee to wait for the car I already own.

CHOOSE YOUR CRITICS
And maybe still ignore them

Somewhere in the process of pushing yourself and your products out into the world you are going to hear from the critics. You may even ask for it. For product development, customer satisfaction, or market testing, you might want to know, "How do you like me so far?"

Be ready to hear the wrong answers.

The first step in getting constructive feedback is to choose your critics wisely. Are they relevant representatives of your target audience? Are they knowledgeable, perceptive and willing to contribute?

You still may not like all the answers. But you should not be asking people who are too complimentary, kind and generous. You want to be surprised or disappointed. To learn something you didn't already know. Maybe you're worrying about the wrong things. You can try to think like a customer, but it's better to ask real customers what they're thinking.

To get valuable feedback from willing critics and retain the right to choose what you use, remember to make two requests at the start:

1. Please be honest, and
2. Please don't be offended, if I choose to ignore your input.

Set the ground rules before your start the game, otherwise somebody's feelings are going to be hurt.

IMAGE IS EVERYTHING

Don't let packaging become a problem

Does your packaging and presentation enhance your competitive advantage? Does it appeal to customers and enhance your brand name? Raise your corporate profile?

Or is it annoying and dysfunctional? Attracting the wrong kind of attention?

The trick is to make packaging decisions in favour of the customer first. Not just for flashy presentation on the shelf or to prevent shoplifting. Think about those packages you hate and make sure you're not among them. Like those giant colourful, appealing boxes of cereal that turn out to be only two-thirds full and the juicy berries are not included. Or the Gillette razor-blades that are locked down and set off alarms if you want to take a closer look.

Is that really helping sales? Making it look overpriced and hard to buy?

Some packaging is all about presentation and not at all practical for consumers when they get it home. Buy a new shirt or pair of socks and you'll ask yourself, *"Why do they need all the paper and cardboard wrapping? And twenty-seven pins buried in painfully hard to find places?"*

And then there's Ketchup. Fifty years of impractical glass bottles that were a challenge to get the tomato paste out of. Was it really a branding strategy to build a cult following of unusually persistent, dedicated buyers? Pissing people off is not usually a good sales tactic. Finally, some genius at Heinz introduced the squeezable upside-down plastic container. Great! And much easier to consume large quantities. Now that has to be good for sales.

How good is your packaging?

Instead of wrapping up your stuff in flashy exaggerated marketing B.S. and tying it down tight so nobody can steal it, think about the higher value of making it functional, appealing, authentic and socially and environmentally responsible. Easy to open, but secure from tampering or inappropriate use. Non-polluting.

And stop worrying about people stealing it. Try giving it away instead.

Those people may just become loyal repeat customers and raving fans who tell everybody how wonderful you and your product are. Those giveaways may be your best-performing marketing initiative.

BAD BEHAVIOUR

Needs to be changed, not explained

Bad behaviour needs to be changed, not analyzed and explained, rationalized or excused.

Speculating over why it's happening may keep the analysts and commentators busy, but it's tiresome and irrelevant. If the bad behaviour can be stopped by removing the cause, then let's do that. If we cannot determine the cause, then let's accept the fact that it will continue unless we change it.

The best way to help change the behaviour is to allow the negative consequences to be evident and obvious to the individual and to his supporters, facilitators and enablers. It doesn't matter if it's an arrogant politician or selfish CEO, delinquent employee or spoiled 5-year old.

Let's learn to change the behaviour or change the player.

(OK, maybe not change your 5-year old. Kids will grow up and behave better, eventually.)

WHAT DID YOU LEARN TODAY?

If your goal is to get better and do better, then you should be learning something new every day. You don't have to be in school to be learning.

There are many alternative learning strategies and they can all make a difference. Read a book, take a course. Go to a training session, workshop, seminar or conference. Share stories with other professionals, entrepreneurs, friends and associates.

You can extract lessons from everywhere and everything that's happening around you, as an observer or as a participant. Lessons on leadership, management, operating effectiveness, personal relations, salesmanship, marketing or customer service. The most valuable lessons are usually free!

Even during the periods when you're relaxing, enjoying your preferred recreation or entertainment activity, pay attention to the strategies, tactics, behaviour and their consequences.

For example, I've found that business is like golf. (See my *Blog: Business is like golf*) The game of golf frequently reminds me of the important basic principles for success: have a strategy and a plan, execute well, stay focused and avoid mistakes.

So back to my initial question, what did you learn today?

POLITICAL DECISIONS

Risky business

Political decisions are risky because they're public and they're personal. They're political because they're about principles, policy and personalities. They're important and unavoidable.

Political decisions have to be made, not just in politics, but also in business and in life. The question is, will the decision be guided by the principles and the policy objectives or by the personalities and the politics in play?

As President John F. Kennedy described in his book, **Profiles in Courage**, the decision maker's courage and character are revealed by decisions that ignore the politics and the personal costs, but defend the most important principles and move everyone in the right direction.

What about political decisions in your business?

Also risky, important and unavoidable. And equally revealing of courage and character. In this book, I've described the Seven Biggest Mistakes that entrepreneurs make and how to avoid them. You may have noted *Mistake #7: Distracted by Personal Issues*.

Personal issues in the business are usually political issues. Especially in family businesses. Company politics often detract from good management and decision making in the business and adversely affect performance. Personalities and political issues may relate to the owner, family members in the business, the management team or some key staff members.

Avoiding the Seven Biggest Mistakes is a question of balance. To avoid Mistake #7, keep your personal objectives in your business plan, but keep personality and petty politics out of your business.

Stick to the important principles.

Be better. Do better.

OPINION VS. ADVICE

Anyone anywhere has the right to an opinion. But don't assume they have any expertise in the subject, even if they pretend they do.

Fake expertise is more dangerous than fake news. Phony experts ranting without any qualifications, knowledge or experience, just VERY LOUD, strong opinions reinforced by the last ignorant idiot they listened to and decided they agree with.

It's the biggest problem with social media and self-published blog posts and articles, it looks like an expert opinion because it's published. But, "I read it on the Internet" should immediately disqualify it from any further consideration, unless a known reputable authoritative source is referenced in the post. Celebrity opinions and endorsements don't count. Rich and famous doesn't make them experts. Look for an expert opinion before you judge or decide.

That's the value of traditional media. We can expect the material to have been fact checked, edited and peer reviewed. And we usually know the biases and political orientation of the publication and the writer.

Turn down the background noise and ignore the raging idiots. High volume and raised emotions are not sufficient to warrant your time and attention. It won't stop them from yelling at you to get your attention, but you can be more selective about who and what you listen to, before forming your own opinion.

Expertise or Opinion. Which is it this time?

If you ask for an opinion you'll get one. Almost nobody can resist giving you a response. They're flattered that you asked and they don't want to disappoint you. Apparently, you think they're an expert in the subject. Or at least you think they might have an intelligent, insightful opinion. Nobody is going to tell you you're wrong, on either count. They're thinking, "Yeah, I'm sure I can come up with something useful." They're never thinking, "But I'm an idiot. I know nothing and have no opinion on the subject." Have you ever heard that answer?

It can be dangerous to ask. What if they're adamant about a really bad idea? Now you have a problem. You cannot respond with, "That's the dumbest thing I ever heard." It's hard to recover from that conversation.

So, carefully select who and how you ask the question and clearly distinguish between a formal request for expert advice and a friendly exchange of personal opinions.

Confirm your expectations before you ask. It will be easier to know what to do with the response.

DEADLINES CAN BE DEADLY
Don't overdo it

Most of us agree that deadlines are necessary. They help us to scope the work and make a plan. Awareness of the deadline helps us to focus and get the work done on time.

But, the stated deadline may be entirely arbitrary or self-imposed and it may actually not be very important at all. Seldom is it absolutely necessary to be on time or you'll be left behind. (Except maybe to catch a flight, make a tee-time or deliver a keynote presentation.)

Deadlines can be helpful until they become an obsession. Then they become a distraction from focusing on the work quality and content. Time is running out and you're not yet finished? You're not yet proud of the work you've done? Re-negotiate the deadline.

Don't obsess over deadlines. Make sure they're real, not arbitrary or imaginary.

PERFECT ENOUGH
Time to expose the flaws

Don't let perfectionism become an excuse for procrastinating. You can continue making improvements, editing, revising, polishing, testing and tuning without ever releasing a final product. But at some point, you have to decide it's perfect enough.

It's time to let fans, readers, customers find the remaining flaws. Maybe they'll love it as it is. They'll never see the same imperfections that you're obsessing over. They may find some that you never noticed.

Let it go. Share your work with the world.

Get to work on the next one. It will start closer to perfection based on what you've already done.

Good enough is too low a threshold, perfect enough is better.

RESULTS ARE ALL THAT MATTER? WRONG
Character matters

Whether you are a CEO, politician, celebrity or simply a humble hard-working entrepreneur or employee, performance is continuously being assessed according to the results you achieve. Does it matter how they are achieved?

Some people think not, results are all that matter. They're wrong.

Character matters.

Ethics, attitude and approach matter. Tactics and methods matter. Success and the desired results may appear to be achieved regardless of the behaviour. Immoral, irresponsible, ruthless and aggressive behaviour may even appear to have been necessary to achieve the results.

Wrong again.

The apparent short-term gains will eventually be lost to long-term reactions. The used and abused will get even. A legacy of accomplishment may be completely ignored, when the true character is revealed.

Just ask Bill Cosby, Harvey Weinstein or Donald Trump.

I HAVE A DUCK

Why do I keep the duck?

It's not a live duck, it's a painted plaster duck, so no care and feeding required. It's old and faded from years in the garden through snow and rain, then sitting beside the bathtub or on a bookshelf. It's not attractive, but it's a helpful reminder to remain humble in my business decisions.

The duck was given to me in a random Christmas gift exchange by a computer technician who worked for me in my first entrepreneurial venture, TTX Computer Products. He was also the first employee I had to fire. Not because of the duck.

It was a classic business slowdown in the industry and it forced me to look at downsizing my staff. "Laid off due to economic circumstances" may sound better to the employer and look better on the employee's resumé, but it is still a difficult and painful decision to fire anyone.

For me it was especially difficult because I had made the commitment never to fire anyone in my own company after having lived through the slow decline and never-ending terminations at my previous employer, right up to my own "lay-off" a few years earlier.

But I came to realize that the best way to protect the company and the jobs of the remaining employees was to accept the inevitable and reduce costs by lowering the most significant variable expense – staff salaries and benefits.

As a senior executive had once assured me, "the only way to avoid ever firing anybody is to make perfect hiring decisions and nobody is that smart." He was right.

It was not the last time for me to have people fired, laid off, or terminated and it never gets easier. I wonder if those CEOs deciding to cut back by 10,000 or 30,000 people take it as personally. Do they actually sit face-to-face with any of those individuals and worry with them about their futures?

It has to be one of the toughest challenges for any entrepreneur or executive. And it's still a worthy objective to try and avoid any firings.

So hire as "perfectly" as you can, then manage well enough to avoid those "economic circumstances" that lead to downsizing.

AND FINALLY, SIMPLE IS NOT ALWAYS WRONG
Maybe it's not that complicated

You've probably seen the frequent Tweets from both Abraham Lincoln and Albert Einstein claiming, *"I never said half that crap you read on the Internet."*

Well, even if Einstein never said it, I like his often quoted comment, *"For every complicated problem there is always an obvious simple solution. That is wrong."*

But maybe he was wrong.

Sometimes the problem is that we make it more complicated than it needs to be. Maybe if we keep it simple, the solution is actually quite simple.

Just a thought. Much as I am reluctant to argue with Einstein.

Please don't Tweet him and get us started.

PART VI
References & Checklists

RECOMMENDED READING FOR MORE WORDS OF WISDOM

In order to help you be better as an entrepreneur, leader, manager and human being, I recommend the following authors for more ideas, information and inspiration. In my opinion, they are among the best at providing thoughtful insights and powerful advice.

I recommend that you make time for them in your process of continuous learning and improvement. Make your own selection from the list below, then find them online, follow them and read their work.

Management Gurus with advice for entrepreneurs

Here are some of their good books and a few memorable quotes:

Tom Peters
In Search of *EXCELLENCE*, 1982

"There is no more important trait among excellent companies than an action orientation. ... if you've got a major problem, bring the right people together and expect them to solve it. They do, somehow, have the time."

"Excellent companies are a vast network of informal, open communications. Forget the MBA - Masters in Business Administration – and remember the MBWA – Management By Walking Around."

Thriving on Chaos, 1987

"A well-handled problem usually breeds more customer loyalty than you had before the negative incident."

"Measure! And reward on the basis of the measures."

Henry Mintzberg
SIMPLY MANAGING, 2013

"*Leadership has pushed management off the map…. Now we are overled and undermanaged.*"

"*Strategies are not immaculately conceived in detached offices. They are learned through tangible experiences.*"

Harvey Mackay
SWIM WITH THE SHARKS without Being Eaten Alive, 1988

"*A goal is a dream with a deadline. Write it down*"

"*Dig your well before you're thirsty*"

"*You'll always get the good news; it's how quickly you get the bad news that really counts.*"

BEWARE THE NAKED MAN WHO OFFERS YOU HIS SHIRT, 1990

"*Do what you love, love what you do and deliver more than you promise.*"

"*You're a lot better off being scared than being bored.*"

Jim Collins
Built to Last, 1994

"*Visionary companies almost religiously preserve their core ideology. Yet, they display a powerful drive for progress that enables them to adapt and change without compromising their cherished core ideals.*"

"*Good enough never is. For these companies the critical question is – How can we do better tomorrow than we did today?*"

From Good to Great, 2001

"*Good is the enemy of great.*"

"*Confront the brutal facts, yet never lose faith.*"

Marcus Buckingham & Curt Coffman
First, Break all the Rules, 1999

"The one insight that we heard echoed by tens of thousands of great managers: People don't change that much. Don't waste time trying to put in what was left out. Try to draw out what was left in. That is hard enough."

Seth Godin
The Bootstrapper's Bible, 2004

"In advertising... persistence is the secret to success."

"In choosing partners remember: Ringo was the luckiest Beatle... a mediocre drummer riding on the backs of three musical geniuses."

Guy Kawasaki
The ART of the START, 2004

"Build a business to make meaning (the money will follow)."

"Have a mantra, not a mission statement."

"Advertising is what you say about yourself, PR is what other people say about you. PR is better."

For some alternative points of view:

Michael Gerber
The E-Myth

Gerber claims he originated the cliché: *Work on your business, not in your business.* But his over-worked theme is a useful reminder to develop your business organisation and processes so that it can run without you in it every day.

Bo Burlingham
Small Giants

An interesting study of small eccentric companies that decided to succeed by staying small. The conclusions are a stretch to fit the hypothesis that small is better, but worth reading to remember to build your business for yourself; not to chase some dream of global grandeur.

FROM AN ENTREPRENEUR OF TWO HUNDRED AND FIFTY YEARS AGO – BENJAMIN FRANKLIN

Perhaps best known as an American statesman and scientist, (he signed the Declaration of Independence, flew a kite in a lightning storm and has his picture on the U.S. $100 bill), Ben Franklin was also a very successful entrepreneur. A printer by trade, he launched several businesses and introduced the concept of franchising to his printing shops. He was successful enough to retire at age forty-two.

He was also a prolific writer and intelligent observer, analyst and commentator on business and life. It is worth considering *Ben Franklin's 12 Rules of Management* by **Blaine McCormick**, © 2000.

In summary:

1. Finish better than your beginnings.
2. All education is self-education.
3. Seek first to manage yourself, then to manage others.
4. Influence is more important than victory.
5. Work hard and watch your costs.
6. Everybody wants to appear reasonable.
7. Create your own set of values to guide your actions.
8. Incentive is everything.
9. Create solutions for seemingly impossible problems.
10. Become a revolutionary for experimentation and change.
11. Sometimes it's better to do 1001 small things right rather than only one large thing right.
12. Deliberately cultivate your reputation and legacy.

More Reading for your personal management issues

To do better in life and manage yourself past the entrepreneurial challenges, these are my recommended reads for personal self-improvement.

The 7 Habits of Highly Effective People, **Stephen Covey**, 1989

"Begin with the end in mind."

"Seek first to understand, then to be understood."

More spiritual than you might expect, but some great insights and tools for personal management.

The 8th Habit, **Stephen Covey**, 2004

A follow-up book presenting the values of *principle centered* leadership.

Awaken the Giant Within, **Anthony Robbins**, 1991

"It is the small decisions you and I make every day that create our destinies."

"It is not events that shape my life and determine how I feel or act, it's the way I interpret and evaluate my life experiences."

The original concepts that launched Tony Robbins and the self-help industry.

The Intelligent Investor, **Benjamin Graham**, 1973

From the professor who taught Warren Buffet how to grow his investments to be worth billions. Buffet calls it *"By far the best book on investing ever written."*

The Wealthy Barber and *The Wealthy Barber Returns*, **David Chilton**, 1989 and 2011

An easier read than Benjamin Graham and a great basic handbook for personal financial management. It should be required reading for every high school student and every investor paying someone else to manage their money.

Any of these books will help you focus on the fundamentals and achieve more successful approaches to your personal growth and development. It's worth finding the time to read them.

And if you have others to recommend I would be pleased to hear from you.

Guiding Principles

As I mentioned in the Introduction, the operating principles for the e2eForum are based on my previous experience with other networking groups, business associations and peer advisory groups.

I recommend these guidelines for you to use in starting your own e2eForum or to improve the effectiveness of a group that you are already participating in.

More than Networking

Most of us have learned the value of a good business or professional network and have promoted our businesses by word-of-mouth marketing through active participation in different networking groups.

These groups usually focus on getting to know new friends and influencers who can help you with leads and referrals. Some groups are more aggressive and structured than others and some members are more annoying and less effective than others; but, much like a typical multi-level marketing organization, they can be very helpful to a new business looking to expand their list of contacts and prospects. They tend to work best for retail and consumer businesses where all the members of the network can become customers of each other, as well as become active sources of leads and referrals.

Industry and professional associations, chambers of commerce and boards of trade can also be valuable resources to build your contact network. However, the networking objective in these groups is usually less explicitly built into the meetings and the group is consequently less valuable as a place to sell your services or request leads and referrals. You will usually need to be more subtle and patient at introducing yourself and your business, while demonstrating your competency and value to other members. Most participants in these groups are turned off by the aggressive networkers who insistently promote their business at every occasion.

Purpose

The e2eForum is structured as a peer advisory group and is much more than a networking group.

You will definitely improve your network of business associates and receive high quality leads and referrals, but the primary purpose of the e2eForum is to learn and share experiences with other entrepreneurs in order to develop better solutions to common challenges and improve business performance.

These are the guiding principles that I recommend for effectively meeting those objectives.

Participation

Membership in the e2eForum is only by invitation from an existing member who has confidence in the capabilities, integrity and suitability of the new member for participation in the meetings. An existing member has the right of veto to exclude any new member, subject only to a required explanation for the inviting member.

Members must all respect the confidentiality of the forum discussions; they must have no personal or business conflict-of-interest; and, they must have no competitive, customer or supplier relationship with any other member.

There are no minimum requirements for time in business, amount of revenue or number of employees. The key criteria are the character of the individual and their ability to contribute to the e2eForum shared learning experience.

New members should receive and accept a confirmation of the principles of operation of the e2eForum.

Group objectives

- Regular interaction with like-minded entrepreneurs who are operating their own business.

- Sharing ideas, information, strategies and operating practices to advance their businesses.

- Developing new business opportunities by exchanging leads and referrals and by direct introduction to new client opportunities.

- Occasional joint efforts to promote their businesses, products and services

Operating Guidelines

- Membership is by invitation only, based on a recommendation by an existing member.

- Maximum of 12-15 members.

- Members are non-competing entrepreneurs in owner-managed businesses.

- Information and exchanges within the group are treated with discretion and respect for client confidentiality.

- No pressure, no quotas, no score-keeping to exchange referrals, leads or introductions to new business.

- No referral fees between members.

- No obligation to do business between members, recognizing the existence of prior relationships, and no obligation to preferential treatment if members become customers or suppliers of each other. (Both of those results will occur naturally, as members get to know, like, respect and trust each other.)

Time, Place and Fees

I recommend morning meetings every three weeks, but alternatively the members may prefer every second week, or only monthly, for example every third Thursday or first Tuesday of every month. (Generally mid-week morning meetings are better for regular attendance, but if day-care drop off or other duties make mornings impossible, then evenings may work better for some groups.)

- Meeting at a convenient hotel or or restaurant that can provide breakfast and a quiet private conference room for the meetings. (Sometimes a member can offer the company board room and provide breakfast services.)
- Meeting agenda scheduled from 7:30 – 9:00AM.
- Membership fees billed semi-annually in advance to cover the costs of the conference room, facilities and breakfast.
- Any special events or e2eForum materials can be included in the semi-annual fees or billed as they occur.
- One member should be designated as the group treasurer to manage the billing and fees.

Agenda

In order for the meetings to be effective and use the limited time effectively, two things are required: **a designated chairperson and an agreed agenda**.

I recommend rotating the chairperson among the experienced members every six months (choosing arbitrarily by seniority or alphabetically, since neither voting nor volunteering ever works very well.)

A meeting agenda for the e2eForum may include any or all of the following items, but typically sections are extended or re-scheduled in order to maintain the 90-minute time limit and provide sufficient time for in-depth discussion on particular issues:

1. Welcome and introduction of guests or new members.

2. Confirm the Agenda and Discussion Points for the day.

3. Member Discussion Forum or Guest Presentation (20 – 40 minutes)

4. Member spotlight (20 – 40 minutes) as an alternative to the standard Discussion Forum or Guest Presentation. Getting to know the member better and sharing advice on current issues.

   • Member's business: Products and services, typical clients and projects.

   • Target Market: type of client, business or industry, typical prospect or primary contacts.

   • Current challenges and opportunities?

   • What can we help you with?

5. Wrap-up Roundtable – Sharing member updates (1 - 2 minutes each, total 15 - 20 minutes).

   • What's new – clients, mandates, milestones?

   • Current issues.

6. Conclude

   • Follow-up action items.

   • Plan for the next meeting.

Events

In addition to the regular meetings, members may also agree to extend their joint efforts to include:

• Meeting on-site for the member Spotlight.

• Organizing an occasional breakfast seminar with invited guests and members presenting themselves and leading the seminar.

• One-on one meetings between members, to develop a closer working relationship and follow-up on any shared opportunities, issues, referrals, leads or other agreed action items.

These guiding principles for operation of the e2eForum will help you to start your own peer advisory group or improve the effectiveness of a group you may already be in.

Discussion Topics

The following section provides some useful discussion topics for any group meeting. In Parts 1, 2 and 3 describing the e2eForum, we covered a number of important discussion topics that are listed below. These are followed by some other suggestions that may be helpful to facilitate additional discussions among the entrepreneurs in your group.

Discussion Topics from the e2eForum

How to succeed in your own business

- When to leap?
- What do you need before you start?
- Who will succeed and who will not?
- Why and why not?

Start-up Decisions

- Strategic Positioning
- Strategic Partnerships
- Business model choices
- Document requirements

Too Entrepreneurial

- Opportunistic
- Optimistic
- Impatient
- Confident
- Decisive
- Creative

The Entrepreneur's Challenge:
- Strategic Leadership + Management Effectiveness

Serial Entrepreneurship
- Another Start-up?
- Or the next Screw-up?

Financial Challenges
- Profit versus Long-term Value
- Managing the Balance Sheet

Key Relationships
- Employees before customers
- Biggest before loudest
- Bankers as partners

Building your Business
- Goal = Long-term, loyal, profitable customers
- Process = Marketing + Sales + Customer Service

Personal Issues
- Family in or out?
- Employees like family?

Preparing for exit
- Establishing business value
- Enhancing business value
- Management succession plans
- Exit strategies

More Suggested Discussion Topics

Recently Read: What did you learn?
- Recommended reading
- Key ideas, principles, recommendations
- How to apply them

Case Studies: Recently in the news
- Big business failure
- Acquisition for big bucks – why?
- Small business success story
- Current business issues being debated

Current Business Challenges
- Employee participation in business ownership
- Compensation plans, incentives, benefits
- Business development – priorities and budgets
- Using Web marketing and social media
- Social responsibility initiatives

CheckLists from the e2eForum

During the e2eForum meetings, Uncle Ralph presented a number of useful Checklists. They are summarized here for easy reference.

Characteristics of a Successful Entrepreneur

- ❑ Energetic, competitive
- ❑ Independent, confident, determined
- ❑ Action-oriented, decisive
- ❑ Passionate, persuasive.

Before you Launch Checklist

- ❑ Skills, knowledge, experience, and contacts relevant to your business plan.
- ❑ Expectations and preferences for the entrepreneurial lifestyle – work routine and environment, prestige and compensation, work/life balance.
- ❑ Personal strengths and weaknesses that will help, not hurt, the business.
- ❑ Healthy foundation – family, physical and financial. Solid or shaky?
- ❑ Strategic resources in place – partners, suppliers, facilities, key customers and employees.
- ❑ Financing for start-up – including your Basic Defensive Interval and the first few months of negative cash flow.

The Start-up Document Checklist

- ❑ Business Plan.
- ❑ Shareholder agreement.
- ❑ Life insurance on each other.
- ❑ Incorporation.

❑ Business licenses and regulatory approvals.

❑ Information systems manuals.

❑ Leases and contracts for facilities and services.

Encore Performance Checklist

Ask yourself these questions before you get started on your next venture:

- What was it that made you succeed in your first business? Did you build your business on your unique management ability, a new product idea, a preferred customer or supplier relationship? Which of these will apply to the new business?

- What mistakes have you avoided in the past? Are you about to make them now? What new risks are you encountering for the first time?

- Is now a good time to start something new? Are there no challenges left in your current business?

- How much will your current business be impacted by a new initiative and the demands on your time and resources?

- Is your past success really transferable to a new business?

Building loyal, long-term, profitable customers

❑ All efforts must be dedicated to the *primary objective of every business: building loyal, long-term, profitable customer relationships*

❑ It's a three-part process of Marketing plus Sales plus Customer Service.

Customer Experience should evolve through four levels:

1. Satisfaction with price and availability

2. Recognition of superior service levels

3. Appreciation of the value of your knowledge and experience

4. Connection on values, mission and vision.

The Six P's of Marketing

Build your marketing objectives and plan around the six P's of marketing strategy and product management.

STRATEGIC:

1. **Positioning**:

    - Strategic positioning of the product relative to competitors in the target market sector will affect all the other elements – placement, promotion, product, pricing, and packaging.
    - Choice of high versus low in quality, price, and service.

2. **Placement**:

    - Where is the product or service available for customers?
    - Choices of retail or wholesale, online or storefront, direct sale or through distributors and sales agents.

3. **Promotion**:

    Choices of priorities, budget and effort in:

    - Direct marketing, advertising.
    - Public relations activities, participation in trade associations, conferences, trade shows.
    - Website, search engine optimisation and web marketing programs.
    - Promotional items, sponsorships.

OPERATIONAL:

4. Product:

- Description of the product or service.
- Features and benefits offered relative to competitors.
- Product development plans to meet changing market demand.

5. Pricing:

- Determined by the market, target market sector, competitors and customer expectations.
- Market price relative to cost is the primary determinant of profitability for the business.
- Volume discounts, incentives, variable pricing?

6. Packaging:

Presentation of the product to the consumer:

- Choices of style, colours and packaging consistent with the corporate image, identity, pricing and performance of the product.
- Warranty, service, accessories, literature, and regulatory requirements?
- Retail display, shipping & handling issues?

The Four P's of Salesmanship

1. Patient
2. Persistent
3. Polite
4. Persuasive

The Seven Biggest Mistakes that Entrepreneurs Make & How to Avoid Them:

1. Too Entrepreneurial
2. Lack of Strategic Direction
3. Focus on Profit
4. Neglecting Key Relationships
5. Poor Marketing and Sales Management
6. "Let's do it again!"
7. Personal Distractions

How to Avoid Them? The Answer is Balance!

Avoiding these mistakes requires the entrepreneur and business owner to:

- o Balance Entrepreneurial Drive with Planning and Analysis
- o Balance Strategic Vision with Operational Detail
- o Balance the Logical Head with the Intuitive Heart
- o Balance Short-term Profit with Long-term Value
- o Balance Personal Priorities with Strategic Objectives.

That completes my list of suggestions on how to learn by sharing stories with other entrepreneurs for ideas, information and inspiration.

Remember to apply what you've learned from this book. A simple concept in a few words:

Avoid the mistakes

Don't Do It the Hard Way

A Personal Note to Readers

Thank you for taking the time to consider my advice and recommendations for building a better business and avoiding the biggest mistakes that entrepreneurs make.

Running a successful business is hard, regardless of how much talent, knowledge and experience you have. It is wise to learn from others and listen to their stories.

I hope these stories have helped you to do better with your own unique challenges whatever they are. You may want to get started in a new business, or to provide better leadership and strategic direction to your business management and growth plans, or to arrange your exit from the business.

DON'T DO IT THE HARD WAY is one of two business books for entrepreneurs I am publishing in 2020. The other book of advice from your Uncle Ralph is titled, **The Complete Do-It-Yourself Guide to Business Plans**. Both books were originally published in 2014.

If you are interested in stories about entrepreneurs, in addition to advice for entrepreneurs, you may also enjoy reading and sharing my Dale Hunter Series of crime fiction novels about a young entrepreneur in the international computer business of the 1980s fighting crime and corruption to save his family and his business. (The stories are similar to my own adventures in business, but it's mostly fiction!) The first three novels in the series were published in 2018 and 2019 – NO EASY MONEY, SIMPLY THE BEST and MERGER MANIAC.

In all my writing, I use storytelling as the best way to share my experience, advice and ideas to help entrepreneurs do better and be better. And to generate a little more sympathy and understanding for entrepreneurs if I can.

I sincerely believe entrepreneurs are capable of making a significant positive contribution to society in spite of the negative popular stereotype of greedy, selfish and irresponsible capitalists. Enlightened entrepreneurs work hard to be better and do better for themselves and their families, their employees, customers and suppliers, their communities and the planet.

All of my writing tries to meet those objectives – to inspire and promote enlightened entrepreneurship.

I hope you enjoy the stories and will recommend the books to your friends. Please share your review comments with me and other readers. It helps us all to make better decisions about what to read and what to write.

You're also invited to visit my websites and join the newsletter mailing lists for the Reader Review Panel or Ideas for Entrepreneurs to keep in touch and receive advance notice of my next writing projects. Please visit: **DelvinChatterson.com** or **LearningEntrepreneurship. com** to sign up.

Many thanks for your continued interest and support of my writing.

Enjoy your reading and learning.

Your Uncle Ralph,

Del Chatterson
Montreal, Canada,
March 2020

ACKNOWLEDGEMENTS

This 2020 Edition of DON'T DO IT THE HARD WAY has been made more valuable, interesting and useful, thanks to the input of all the clients, consultants, bankers, business partners, investors and associates that I have worked with during the last thirty years and more. I could not possibly name them all. Some may recognize themselves in the stories I've told and I apologize if they remember it differently or if I neglected to mention all the lessons we learned together.

I also appreciate and respect all the feedback and suggestions from readers, friends and associates on the earlier editions. They have contributed immensely to making this 2020 Edition a better resource for entrepreneurs.

The quality of the final publication has been greatly enhanced by the active support and professional services for the book cover and interior design by Rodolfo Borello and the publishing, printing and fulfilment services of Canam Books/Rapido Press.

And most importantly, thank you to my infinitely patient wife, Penny Rankin, who used to be suspicious of entrepreneurs and has now supported and encouraged me through every revision of all my business books in support of enlightened entrepreneurship.

Thank you all!

Your Uncle Ralph,

Del Chatterson

Montreal, Canada,

March 2020

The Author, Delvin R. Chatterson

Del Chatterson is dedicated to helping entrepreneurs to be better and to do better. He is an experienced entrepreneur and executive, business advisor, consultant, coach, writer and cheerleader for entrepreneurs.

Del provides ideas, information and inspiration to business owners, managers and entrepreneurs around the world through his consulting business, DirectTech Solutions, his website at **LearningEntrepreneurship.com** and his books, articles and posts on social media.

Originally from the Rocky Mountains of British Columbia, Del has lived and worked for most of the past forty years in the fascinating, multicultural, bilingual, French-Canadian city of Montreal, Quebec. He has helped entrepreneurs around the world, including volunteer consulting and financial support for developing economies and Indigenous communities. His own life experience includes running nine marathons after the age of fifty (setting no records, but never being last) and running for Member of Parliament in the 2000 Canadian federal election. (He came second, not last.)

In addition to his business books, Del is writing fiction with the Dale Hunter Series of crime thrillers about an entrepreneur in Montreal in the international computer business of the 1980s (Not his true life story. It's mostly fiction, he says.) He is also working on a collection of short stories.

Del has helped businesses at all stages: from start-up through to the operating and management challenges of achieving sustainable growth and the exit strategies for management transition and succession plans. His expertise is most often applied in assessing business performance and developing strategic plans to achieve improvements.

Del has lectured at Concordia and McGill Universities on entrepreneurship, financial management and business planning. He has given seminars and workshops on business management and entrepreneurship issues and continues to offer his advice for entrepreneurs through his Blogs, articles and books under the persona of Uncle Ralph.

Del Chatterson is an engineer from the University of British Columbia with an MBA from McGill University. He started a computer products distribution business, called TTX Computer Products, in 1986 and grew it to $20 million in annual sales with distribution centres in Montreal and Boston in eight years. He then took it into a merger to expand the business across Canada. The merger was eventually wound up as the computer industry rapidly evolved to become more concentrated around a few major players and Del transitioned to the new economy of Internet and Web based businesses.

Del is a valuable resource to business managers and entrepreneurs in a wide array of businesses for his strategic insights, perceptive assessments and insightful analysis of business performance and for defining action plans to realize opportunities for improvement.

You can learn more about Del at his author website: **DelvinChatterson.com** and more of his advice for entrepreneurs at: **LearningEntrepreneurship.com**. You may also follow him on Twitter, Facebook, Instagram, or LinkedIn.

Thank you for sharing his books and providing your feedback, comments, and reviews. Del welcomes any opportunity to connect with his readers, fans and friends and appreciates your support.

* * * * *